Finishing STRONG

An Estate Planning Journey

Ronald "Skip" Skolnik &
Elizabeth "Libby" Skolnik Budweg

Finishing Strong
An Estate Planning Journey
Copyright © 2023 by Ronald "Skip" Skolnik and Elizabeth "Libby" Skolnik Budweg

Published by Lucid Books in Houston, TX
www.LucidBooks.com

All rights reserved. No part of this publication may be reproduced, stored in a retrieval system, or transmitted in any form by any means, electronic, mechanical, photocopy, recording, or otherwise, without the prior permission of the publisher, except as provided for by USA copyright law.

ISBN: 978-1-63296-983-5
eISBN: 978-1-63296-631-5

Special Sales: Most Lucid Books titles are available in special quantity discounts. Custom imprinting or excerpting can also be done to fit special needs. Contact Lucid Books at Info@LucidBooks.com

Disclaimer: The material presented in this book is for informational, illustrative, and educational purposes and does contain some hypothetical examples. Certain information has been obtained from third-party sources considered to be reliable but is not guaranteed that such information is accurate or complete. You should consult with a licensed professional for advice concerning your specific situation.

No part of this book may be reproduced, stored in a special system, or transmitted, in any form or by any means, electronic, mechanical, photocopying, recording or otherwise without prior permission from the publisher.

DEDICATION

As I look back on my life, experiences, and career, I see many influences that have made me who and what I am today. The value of a strong, stable home life in our formative years can never be understated. This truly is the greatest gift people can give their children. It helps children develop well when they're in a confident, safe, and supportive environment. My parents, Ron and JoAnne, provided that for me. Then as I grew and developed, they provided an incredibly stable and fun environment that gave me opportunities to learn and grow. These avenues included the Scouting program, travel, and the freedom to chart my own course.

I'd also like to give my heartfelt thanks to my family and friends who have had (and still have) a substantial influence on my life. It has been said that you are the average of your five closest friends. The friends I have had the privilege of enjoying life with are an impressive lot. Being associated with them is an honor. They have encouraged me and been supportive through thick and thin.

And of course it goes without saying that I need to thank Amy, my loving, patient wife and life partner. Her capacity to care is unrivaled. She has been by my side supporting and encouraging me through all of life's mountaintops and valleys. The life we created for ourselves has had and will continue to have incredible high points. But when we've encountered the not-so-great times, she has proudly been by my side and supported me. My thanks and love for her will never end.

I dedicate this book and its lessons to all these important people.

-Skip

TABLE OF CONTENTS

FOREWORD	i
INTRODUCTION	1
Chapter One ESTATE PLANNING	15
Chapter Two THE "BIG FOUR" ISSUES	27
Chapter Three LEGAL PLANNING (OR HOW MOST PEOPLE SEE ESTATE PLANNING)	39
Chapter Four OUR PROCESS FOR NURSING HOME PROTECTION	47
Chapter Five OUR PROCESS FOR PROTECTING ASSETS	67
Chapter Six LIFE'S CLOSING CHAPTER	73
Chapter Seven NEXT STEPS	77
Chapter Eight EAT THE CAKE, TAKE THE TRIP	89
CONCLUSION	95

FOREWORD

Friends, family, and clients asked why we're working so hard on this next book. The truth is that just like everything at our firm, it needs to be done. Every day we're astounded by the level of unpreparedness we see in many facets of life, but especially in estate planning.

Life is a cycle. We are born and raised, we reproduce, we live our lives and enjoy our time here, and then we eventually decline and pass away. Yes, we each have our own paths, but when it comes to the cycle of life, there should be no surprises. Yet people seem shocked when life happens, particularly bad things. However, we personally believe that it is our responsibility as husbands, wives, parents, grandparents, and great-grandparents to take care of business—even the bad stuff. That's probably why we do what we do.

The whole concept of a comprehensive estate plan is to make sure that if something bad happens, there is a plan to offset, mitigate, avoid, or have a roadmap to navigate the problem. Still, there are two major problems with estate planning.

The first is that people don't see a problem having an estate plan that isn't comprehensive. And let's be honest, you can't fix a problem if you don't acknowledge its existence. People always want to do what they have always done. They save for a while and think they're prepared, but then they turn 84 and spend a big chunk of their assets on nursing home costs. As we'll show you, that's vastly avoidable if you plan ahead.

Some of the families we meet understand the importance and priority of a comprehensive estate plan. But those folks are in the minority. Most think it will just work out fine, like it's magic or something. This is unacceptable to us. Yes, everything could work out. But more often, problems arise, and a lack of preparation leaves a family's loved ones in a rat's nest of legal, financial, and emotional garbage. Again, it could easily be avoided with some time and effort spent on putting things in order.

Here are some indications that you might be unprepared in estate planning:

- Not having the necessary legal documents
- Not having assets positioned properly from a financial perspective
- Not having a plan to avoid or mitigate nursing home costs
- Not having a plan to avoid probate court
- Not having a plan to efficiently disperse assets as you want
- Not having a plan to reduce taxes
- Not having a plan for your final wishes (including funerals)

The second issue is that people don't know where to begin to put together a comprehensive estate plan. What typically happens is that they meet with an attorney (likely someone who helped them get out of a traffic ticket), transfer some property, or do some other task not related to estate planning.

The legal profession has become very specialized, much like the medical profession. Would you see a general practitioner for brain surgery? Of course not. Even if the attorney is really good, without the specialized knowledge of estate planning, the guidance comes from only one perspective. That's not a comprehensive approach, and important things could be missed.

There are eight very specific skill sets that must work together in concert to truly have a successful and comprehensive estate plan. And while it might seem like a lot of work, it's what's required to "Finish Strong" in the last third of your life and leave the legacy you want.

INTRODUCTION

We're getting older as a country.

Never before has such a large portion of the US population been over 65 years old. In fact, the over-65 crowd will make up 20 percent of all Americans by 2030. At that point, experts say that demand for health care and other support services will outpace supply, making costs escalate.

> The start of the 2030s will mark a turning point for demographics in the US, particularly for the elderly population, according to the US Census Bureau's 2017 National Population Projections. By 2030, every Baby Boomer will be age 65 or older, which means that 1 out of every 5 Americans will be of retirement age.
>
> —*Insider Intelligence, January 1, 2023*

Most Americans think they're prepared for the cost of aging. But the hard truth is that they're not. We know that to be true because the majority of people who walk into our estate planning practice aren't prepared. But they think they are.

What does "prepared" mean? It means you've thought through the remainder of your life. You've figured out what all the risks are and how much things will cost. Finally, it means you've determined how you'll address these costs and are actively working to preserve and protect the assets you'll need in retirement.

This book will cover many topics, but it will mainly focus on how to protect yourself from lawsuits, probate, nursing home costs, and market fluctuations as you age. All these things can derail your plans and negatively affect your family. We'll also discuss typical problems families face in estate planning and why too many people avoid estate planning despite how simple many of these problems are to solve.

Putting together a modern, comprehensive estate plan initially requires a tremendous amount of research. It includes reviewing your income, expenses, investments, savings, and insurance coverage (life, property, and casualty policies). But we don't stop there.

The research is just the beginning. We also cover the eight essential perspectives that need to be addressed in estate planning. Then we bring together a team of professionals with expertise in these areas to work on your behalf. They include attorneys, accountants, financial planners, insurance professionals, nursing home specialists, and funeral directors. Your estate planning team then helps develop a personalized plan just for you and your family.

Estate planning at this level is both an art and a science. The science is that there are specific and complex requirements from tax, legal, investment, and nursing home perspectives. The art of the estate plan is weaving a successful path within the bounds of all the rules and regulations.

Of course, we'll dive into what estate planning can cost. More importantly, if working with an estate planner isn't in your budget, we'll give you enough information to take on the more essential tasks yourself. After all, if it's not affordable, it's not a solution.

Most of all, we'll talk about the outcomes of a good estate plan and how that can have a positive impact on your family. When done right, estate plans provide families a sense of comfort and ease so everyone gets along during potentially tough times.

Your estate plan is your legacy. Whether it's support for your spouse, gifts to your favorite causes, leaving something for the next generations, or anything else, the choices you make during the planning process reflect your core values and beliefs.

So it's critical to have your desired "end picture" in mind. We want to give you clarity because what really matters is that you have a complete and comprehensive plan in place to protect your finances and your family.

Before we get started, meet our executive team: Ron "Skip" Skolnik and Elizabeth "Libby" Skolnik Budweg.

AN INTRODUCTION TO SKIP

SKOLNIK RETIREMENT SOLUTIONS

The Early Days

Skip grew up in the Northfield/Macedonia area, which is between Cleveland and Akron Ohio. He attended Nordonia High School he continued his education at Otterbein College. Skip was active in the Drama and the Scouting Program where he achieved the rank of Eagle Scout.

For many, being a Boy Scout was just an adolescent phase, an extracurricular activity. But for me, it was a transformative achievement that began when I was 10 and formally ended when I turned 18. But the experience still shapes my life today.

I can still hear the Scoutmaster helping us recite these familiar words:

> *On my honor, I will do my best to do my duty to God and my country and to obey the Scout Law;*
>
> *To help other people at all times;*
>
> *To keep myself physically strong, mentally awake, and morally straight.*

I liked that Scouting was a structured environment with specific rules and benchmarks for success. It agreed with me. By age 17 I achieved the rank of Eagle Scout. If I look at the world of estate planning that I've worked hard to master today, I can see the parallels to Scouting.

The second set of experiences that formed my life occurred during my time in Lakeside, Ohio. My family began vacationing there when I was eight years old. In that safe community, my big brother and I had tremendous freedom to roam and become educated about life. We learned how people should act and how we should treat them. Since the community was faith-based, we were taught important values in a magical environment.

Once we were old enough, summers in Lakeside offered plenty of opportunities to work at a job we liked, and I liked sailing. With my Red Cross certification in hand, I worked my way up the sailing instructor ladder each summer and kept working there even into my college years.

I'm glad I did because that was when I met Amy. She was the nice park director who was two years older than I was—an intimidating fact when you're just 19. But I knew soon after meeting her that she was the girl I was going to marry. The following summers and "not summers" were filled with growing romance and lots of long letters (that was back when you had to pay for long distance phone calls and before the Internet). Eventually I mustered up the courage to ask her father for her hand in marriage. Thank God I kept working in Lakeside!

Naturally, we were married at the gazebo overlooking Lake Erie in Lakeside, about 100 yards from where we first met. That setting has been the backdrop of the greatest adventure I've ever experienced—creating a life with Amy and raising our two lovely "lake girls," Abbey and Libby. We've been lucky enough to be accompanied by the friends we made as kids who still visit every summer.

INTRODUCTION

The ensuing years were and continue to be full and rich. And many of us will eventually retire to live full-time in Lakeside.

Life Lessons Learned through Hardship

Of course, like most people, life has also thrown a few unexpected curveballs my way. However, they helped form who I am today.

As a boy, I loved spending time with my Grandpa Mitchell. He always found time for us, taught us, and showed us how to live. But I was shocked—and felt cheated—when he died before I had the chance to show him who I would become.

When our firstborn made her grand entrance into the world, the joyous occasion was marred by an incident that meant she would spend a week in a neonatal intensive care unit on 24-hour watch. Despite the touch-and-go start, she grew into a healthy child, but not without countless prayers.

And then my business partner who helped build our successful advertising business had some dangerous addictions that led to his arrest. It almost forced us into financial ruin.

But I gleaned some important lessons from those bad times. I learned from my grandfather that our time on earth is finite—life doesn't go on forever. With our daughter Abbey, I learned to trust in God—we are ultimately not in control. And my former business partner's issues taught me that there is evil in the world, so we must choose wisely and seek out the good.

There have been other life lessons as well. My sailing instructor days taught me to relate and communicate with all types of people. In addition, my passion for the sport of sailing taught me that you're never done learning; it's a lifelong journey.

A Career with Purpose

I was lucky to have a hard-working father who excelled at sales and entrepreneurship. I learned a lot from him. Soon after college and a few false starts, I launched a small business with Amy that eventually grew into a full-scale advertising agency. One major client was a successful estate planning attorney. The extensive research I did for this client introduced me to the senior market.

After some unexpected twists and turns, I found myself in the funeral home business. But I was again focusing on the needs of a primarily senior citizen population. In time, I grew my role from funeral preplanning to helping with all aspects of the families' lives I served as they entered their senior years.

I realized that two things drove me in life: passion and seeing people do what they're "supposed to be doing." I took it upon myself to become an expert in how best to serve this population. Soon after, I was making a real impact on how my clients would live out the rest of their days with peace of mind and protection.

After working with hundreds of families and studying the senior market for more than 20 years, I came to a sound conclusion—everybody entering their golden years should focus on three key things:

- Financial readiness
- Legal preparation
- Funeral preplanning

I became a retirement planning professional with a three-pronged goal: (1) to protect people's assets from nursing care expenses, (2) to preserve the assets so they outlast the owners, and (3) to position assets so the next generation can inherit them efficiently and with the lowest possible tax burden.

INTRODUCTION

My life's work is to educate and change the perception of retirement planning—to take it from fantasy to reality. That includes providing a direction, a plan, and a road map for each client's particular circumstances.

My daughter Libby and I wrote this book to expand that approach to many more people. I want everyone to be able to benefit from my personal motto: "Finish Strong!"

AN INTRODUCTION TO LIBBY

SKOLNIK RETIREMENT SOLUTIONS

I joined the family advisory firm because I love helping people. It's always been a big part of who I am. Now I'm doing some of the most important work in our clients' lives— helping them achieve their financial goals and live well in retirement.

There are many pathways I can take being in the financial industry. My focus is on multifaceted estate plans. I hold multiple insurance licenses and securities registrations, which allow me to help people develop and implement a comprehensive plan that fits their estate planning needs.

One of my specialties is to offset, mitigate, or provide a path to navigate any financial roadblocks or unexpected problems that may arise during the golden years. Not everything always goes according to plan. Sometimes unforeseen issues pop up. But like my dad, I understand the value of preparation. I also like to acknowledge the fact that sometimes you have to pivot to achieve your retirement goals. I have a personal mission of always learning and improving, and that extends to our clients.

I'm constantly educating and working diligently to help clients understand the ins and outs of their plans. I strongly believe that in order for our clients to achieve their goals, they need to understand their financial choices and the strategies that will help get them where they want to go. Like my dad, I embraced the exciting and ever changing world. I have had the privilege of traveling all over this beautiful country and internationally (I even lived in Slovenia at one point). My husband, Stephen, and I are avid travelers, always looking to explore. We also enjoy cooking and attending classic car shows. Our faith is important to us, first and foremost. I volunteer with our church's international student ministries program, kids ministry & we have had the opportunity to be a part of international missions trips around the world. I'm extremely passionate about faith, family, and making a positive, lasting impact on the lives of others.

I previously worked with a technology company, having the experience of managing accounts across the state of Ohio. Education was the key to success when it came to the use of technology. This equates to the education and understanding of the tools we use in estate planning. It is essential that I take into consideration and stay up to date with all the rules and regulations I deal with daily to make sure my clients get the highest quality services possible. I take this very seriously and I want to make sure every family understands what their plan involves and how it works in favor of preparing and protecting them.

I've had the privilege of working with many local community organizations and had the privilege to witness the impact they have made in areas where I not only live currently, but have grown up in as well. A great example of an organization I've had the opportunity to be a part of is Leadership Lorain County. With my participation through this wonderful organization I was able to grow my personal and professional developmental skills. I also sat on the Board of

INTRODUCTION

Directors for the Community Foundation of Lorain County. Along with my leadership experience, board training, teamwork, communication and community awareness that leverages my skill set in the role I currently fill as a financial planner for Skolnik Retirement Solutions. I'm committed to my own development and attribute my success to self-discipline and bringing enthusiasm to every aspect of life. These varied interests, experiences, and passions give me a unique perspective that helps me develop personalized estate plans for our clients families. I love what I do and am eager to help.

What we're explaining in this book comes from 20 years of experience in the senior market. First, it offers an overview of what we do and how we help families every day. From there, we tell three specific stories that represent big trends we see with the people we serve (note: we have not used their real names).

You may know people who have been down the estate planning path. You might have heard horror stories and about times when things worked out well. In this book, we want to provide some examples to personalize the planning process. Our motivations are to help you understand the true cost of not planning and show you how to avoid that fate.

FIRST, HERE'S THE STORY OF MARK

Mark was a local veteran who found himself in a horrible situation. At 60, he was a widower with three kids. After a nearly three-decade career at a Ford plant in Ohio, he had a few dollars saved up and was living an average retirement. While retired, he met his friends at a local restaurant every Tuesday for breakfast. After one of those meals on a particularly cold and blustery day, he left the restaurant in a hurry. Unfortunately, Mark was in a bad car crash and was found responsible. Three people were seriously injured. One of them was Mark. His steering wheel slammed into his chest, fracturing his ribs and puncturing a lung. The crash left Mark in critical condition.

Not long after, Mark passed away. His insurance covered some of the liabilities, but the lawsuit that ensued exceeded his asset value. His brokerage account was forced to liquidate. As a result, Mark's three kids got nothing to honor his 28-year career and four years of service in the Army.

Mark's story is sad. It is also completely avoidable.

NEXT, LET'S TALK ABOUT BOB AND JEAN.

Bob was age 72, and Jean was 70. They were married for 52 years and had five kids. Bob was a successful, educated businessman. By all accounts, Bob and Jean were living the "American Dream." They were high school sweethearts and went to Bowling Green State University together. Bob went on to get a graduate degree from Ohio State University. They came back to their hometown in rural Ohio, and Bob joined his father-in-law's small garage-based business that he then grew to a successful enterprise with more than 20 employees.

One day Jean was not feeling well and visited her doctor. Unfortunately, she was diagnosed with pancreatic cancer and passed away just four months later. Obviously, that was a stressful time for the family. But it was made worse by fighting about how the funeral should be handled—burial or cremation—and where the funeral would take place. All the ensuing arguments led to more stress in the family.

Fast forward a few years. Bob was on his way to work but became confused and pulled over to the side of the road. When the police found him, they took him to the emergency room. Soon after, he was diagnosed with Alzheimer's disease and could no longer stay at his home. He was admitted to a nursing home for his own safety and lived there 29 months until he passed away. At $10,000 per month, the nursing home costs totaled almost $300,000. His kids were forced to sell the family home and liquidate assets to cover these costs.

Bob and Jean were educated and smart. They thought they were prepared. However, you now know that they were not. There was infighting between the kids about who should handle Bob's medical care and personal business affairs. Neither Bob nor Jean made these decisions, and after his diagnosis, Bob wasn't able to make them himself. The kids also argued about who should be responsible for running Bob's successful business. Since Bob and Jean weren't prepared with wills and other advanced directives, the remainder of their estate had to go through probate, which the family wasn't expecting. So the business was liquidated. And when all was said and done, the five kids were left with only about $9,000 each out of an estate that was valued at close to $1 million.

Even worse, the kids don't talk to each other anymore. Money is one thing; broken relationships are another. When you realize this could have been sidestepped by having some simple documents in place, it hurts even more.

Again, all this was completely avoidable. Bob and Jean thought they were prepared, but they weren't. They were smart people who just didn't finish the estate planning process.

The third story is about Brenda and Mike. But we'll save their story for later because they're an example of what things look like when you plan ahead and are prepared. They addressed everything we're going to discuss in this book before it was too late. It's the ultimate example of the "Finish Strong" motto.

Failing to plan has real costs. They can come in the form of delayed care and additional legal fees. Bob and Jean wasted $500,000 in their situation. Families can also endure larger tax liabilities on inherited retirement accounts if they're not structured correctly. Additionally, there can be stress and anguish for the surviving spouse (Bob had to live with that).

Most importantly, in Bob and Jean's situation, not having a comprehensive estate plan cost the children their relationships with each other. Since things weren't decided clearly and with cool heads in advance, the kids fought, eventually ceasing contact altogether.

Again, this was all completely avoidable.

Real problems compound when people don't pay attention to estate planning until it's too late. Then, instead of leaving a great legacy, they might leave only breadcrumbs to those they care about most.

THE COST OF NOT PLANNING

Failing to plan has *real* cost

Delayed Care

Additional Legal Fees

Over $500,000 Wasted

Higher Taxes

Stress and Anguish on the surviving spouse

Broken Relationships between the kids

Chapter One

ESTATE PLANNING

The real issue with estate planning isn't that no one ever thinks about it. We've had a pandemic that reminds us daily of our vulnerability. And our TV screens are filled with medicines for seemingly every disease, reverse mortgage loans to afford our lifestyles, and settlement offers to pull money out of life insurance policies.

The real issue is that people don't understand the problem completely. They think there's one single issue: an estate plan.

Underestimating the Scope of the Problem

Estate planning is like the mythical Hydra. In Greek and Roman mythology, the Hydra was a terrible, multi-headed beast that would come down from the mountains to destroy villages and people. The villagers would send their greatest warrior out to defend them. However, this warrior would have only a single weapon—a long blade. Worse, if he was skilled enough to lop off one of the beast's heads, another head would grow back in its place.

Strangely enough, estate planning is similar. A complete estate plan has eight perspectives that must be addressed simultaneously and in concert with each other. Yet the average American tries to accomplish estate planning goals with a single tool, just like the warrior who fought the Hydra.

Like the Hydra, there are multiple perspectives to estate planning.

1. Legal protection
2. Financial protection
3. Legacy
4. Tax reduction
5. Health care
6. Income planning
7. Nursing home protection
8. Funeral planning

The hard part is that all these must work together to provide the best protection. For example, we have a new client who was working with a prominent attorney before seeing us. The client received good advice; however, it was only from the legal perspective. Failing to consider the other seven estate planning perspectives created a huge tax issue for the surviving spouse and children. All eight estate planning perspectives must be considered when making a plan and carrying it out.

Our entire firm is designed around the idea of creating a comprehensive estate plan. We bring in professionals for each estate planning area to research, develop, design, and implement complete plans for our clients.

STATISTICS DON'T LIE...

70% of people now age 65 and older will need some period of extended care during the remainder of their life.

U.S. News and World Report, November 2018

As much as we'd like to ignore the facts, statistics don't lie. We have some real problems in our country today.

Seven out of 10 Americans now age 65 or older will need some period of extended care during their lives. Admittedly, this could be something like a short-term rehabilitation for a knee or hip replacement (and Americans get a lot of these). Or it could be like what happened to members of our family. Amy's mother spent almost seven years in a facility, and Skip's grandmother had a 14-year stay.

Let's look at some more statistics.

STATISTICS DON'T LIE...

67% of people don't have a will.

Caring.com January 2020

STATISTICS DON'T LIE...

86% of people think estate planning is important but don't know where to begin.

AARP, August 2019

73% of people have no advanced directives

US News and World Report, November 2018

MY OBSERVATION:

100% of people believe... "It won't happen to me!" But it does!

Despite the recent pandemic, 67 percent of people in this country don't have a will. And while 86 percent of Americans think estate planning is essential, they don't know where to begin. Meanwhile, 73 percent of folks have no advanced directives in place such as a living will or a durable power of attorney for health care. Their decisions about end-of-life care essentially are up in the air.

It's clear there are some unprepared people out there. Don't be one of them.

STATISTICS DON'T LIE...

87% of people now age 65 have no plan for long-term care.

US News and world Report, November 2018

Then there's the issue of long-term care. Right now, 87 percent of people ages 65 and older have no plan for long-term care. In our two decades of experience working with families, our observation is this: 100 percent of people don't believe it will happen to them. Yet it does, and they're unprepared.

Being Average = Making Mistakes (Don't Be Average!)

The average person does estate planning the wrong way. They plan to the best according to their abilities but without full knowledge.

They might call the attorney who helped their brother get out of a traffic ticket. They'll get one perspective, but it's probably off base. You see, most attorneys are specialized. Unless they do estate planning daily, they're not going to have the perspective to know what needs to be done.

Someone else might call their accountant or their financial advisor. Or they might call one of their friends who knows even less than they do. The problem is that they're getting limited information from people who lack a broad perspective.

Even if these folks know what they're talking about, it's from only one perspective. The accountant doesn't know the legal side. The financial person doesn't know the accounting side, and so forth. It's a real issue because each expert needs to work in concert with all the other experts. That's why we use a completely holistic approach to estate planning involving specialists from the legal, financial, insurance, and funeral director fields.

THE AVERAGE PERSON DOES ESTATE PLANNING THE WRONG WAY

Attorney

Financial Advisor

Accountant

Friends & Family

Estate planning isn't just end-of-life planning. It's not just the last phase before you say your final goodbyes. Proper estate planning begins before retirement. Well-designed estate plans account for what happens after you're gone from legal, family, and financial perspectives. The process is dynamic and results in a plan that ensures some key things.

- You will have adequate income in retirement
- You're prepared to retire from an investment perspective
- You have the necessary estate documents in place
- You have backup plans if something bad happens

Our goal for you is to have a team that possesses expertise in these areas to help develop and implement an estate plan that helps you achieve your retirement vision. We've done our job if the plan is flexible and creates a path for the smoothest, easiest transition for you and your loved ones.

These parts of life need to be planned. Yet most people just wing it and hope it turns out okay. But we don't want just "okay" for you; we want something spectacular.

Our office has been helping people with estate planning for more than two decades. The team we've assembled is incredibly talented and skilled in working with families. We have a different perspective than other planners. You'll see how it all fits together.

Our perspective isn't just a collection of ideas pulled together by a few people. Our firm is part of a professional network of hundreds of experts covering 38 states across the country. The tools, tactics, and strategies we use for estate planning are applied successfully throughout the United States.

Our organization is nationally recognized for successful estate planning. While that's nice, it's not why you should keep reading. What's more important is that we're passionately obsessed with making sure people are prepared (a nod to Skip's Eagle Scout background).

We're amazed at how many people have not taken important initial steps in estate planning. For example, not long ago we spoke to a local senior group at a restaurant. A well-dressed couple in their mid-80s, Ralf and Audrey, were joined by their daughter Cindy who was furiously taking notes. After the presentation, she was the first to have her hand up and ask questions. Some were personal in nature, so we invited them to sit down at our office to have their questions answered.

About a week later, Cindy and her father came in, just the two of them. We asked if Audrey was doing well. Tearing up, Cindy said her mom was at a local nursing home and wouldn't be attending our meetings. We helped as much as we could, but fast forwarding to the present, Audrey is still on needed care in a facility that costs more than $11,500 per month. Under the circumstances, it's money well spent. However, imagine if 10 years ago the family had taken the time to prepare for the common things that can happen to people in their 80s. Audrey would still get all the care she needs at most any facility she wanted, but all of the family's assets that were collected over the last 60 years would be protected and passed on to the kids and grandkids rather than spent on necessary care.

This is one of the biggest problems in estate planning and nursing home protection in particular. There is a path to protection. The issue is that you have to know about it and put the plan in place five years before it's needed.

This situation is why we're obsessively passionate about estate planning. Too many people are very unprepared, and it runs the gamut—from not having the basic required medical directives in place to ignoring funeral preplanning, to not understanding the complexities of nursing home protection.

Our mission is to help. We have three primary objectives.

Objective No. 1

We want to help protect and preserve assets from lawsuits, probate, nursing home costs, and market fluctuations.

Objective No. 2

We aim to simplify and consolidate your financial and legal worlds. This process may seem easy when families are still mentally sharp. But as you know, when we approach 70, 80, 90, and beyond, things that were once easy begin to feel complicated.

As Americans, we tend to demand two things: choice and control. When things are simplified and consolidated, it's easier to control our worlds and dictate our destinies.

Objective No. 3

We seek to maximize, multiply, and distribute assets in a straightforward, uncomplicated, and tax-advantaged manner. It doesn't matter where you want your legacy to go; we want it to be simple, easy, and safe from predatory taxes.

OUR MISSION

1. Preserve and Protect Assets from:
- Lawsuits
- Probate Court
- Nursing Home Costs
- Market Fluctuations

2. Simplify and Consolidate your stuff

3. Maximize and Multiply then distribute your assets when you are done with them in a way that is:
- Simple
- Easy
- And in a Tax-advantaged manor

WE ARE LASER FOCUSED — **SKOLNIK RETIREMENT SOLUTIONS**

Let's go back and look at how Bob and Jean's end-of-life experience could have been different if estate planning had been done right. When Jean passed away, the funeral should have been preplanned years in advance. If so, there would have been no arguments or discussions among the family members.

When Bob fell ill, advanced directives should have been in place. Then there would have been no question about who had guardianship or what was going to happen.

Proper estate planning is a "must" for several reasons—to protect assets from the nursing home, to avoid inheritance taxes, to protect assets from any market downturns, and to ensure that nothing ever goes to probate.

That would have been an estate plan done right. But it didn't turn out that way for Bob and Jean's family, and it often doesn't for many others because people don't pause to consider their situations, and in turn don't act. Years prior, Bob and Jean needed to bring in a specialist who could help them protect their assets. They didn't do that, and the inaction was costly.

A recent AARP survey[1] found this:

A vast majority (86%) of nonretired adults ages 40-64 recognize that preparing for retirement is important. However, this belief doesn't seem to motivate people to prepare, as evidenced by the numbers who feel they are not as prepared as they should be.

Estate planning might seem complicated. But to help families through it, we developed a comprehensive planning system that addresses every critical perspective families need to consider. We mentioned it earlier, referring to how estate planning is like the mythical monster Hydra with multiple heads that all need to be tamed at once.

It's called the OctaView Retirement System™. For every family we work with, we look at their unique situation through eight lenses.

---

[1] *https://www.aarp.org/pri/topics/work-finances-retirement/financial-security-retirement/planning-successful-retirement.html#:~:text=A%20vast%20majority%20(86%25),prepared%20as%20they%20should%20be by Carmenza Millan and Colette Thayer, AARP Research Published November 15, 2022 Viewed: Aug 2023*

Our Solution to the Planning Problem: **OctaView Retirement System**™

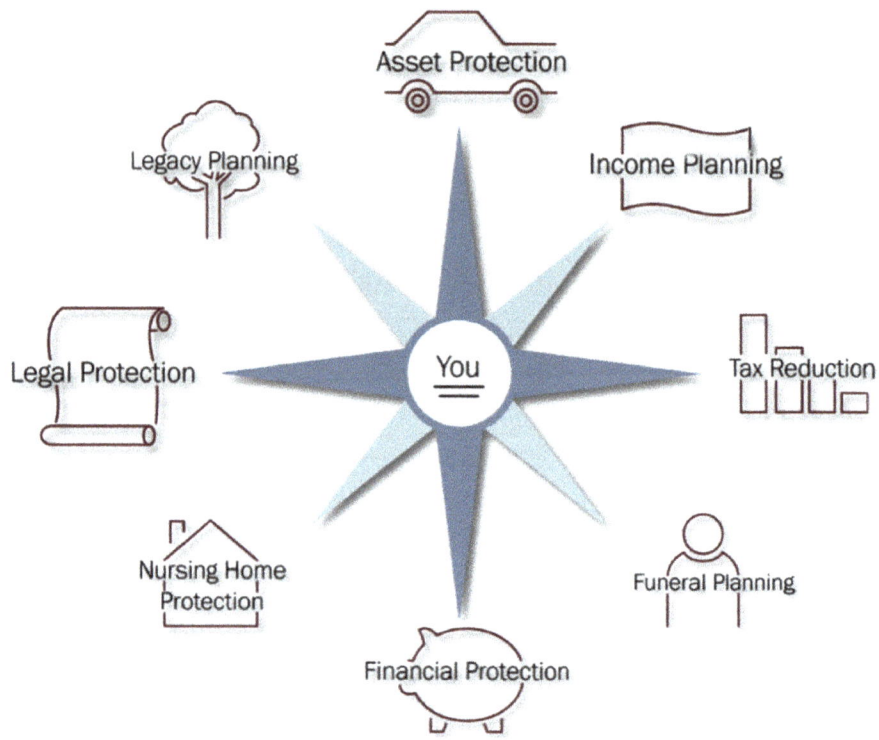

Of course, all these estate planning aspects are important. But you have to start somewhere. The next chapter focuses on the most essential areas, or what we call the "Big Four."

Chapter Two

THE "BIG FOUR" ISSUES

Before looking at the Big Four issues, let's look at some context regarding these four primary financial phases of life: dependent, accumulation, preservation, and distribution. They set the stage for the Big Four.

Life's Financial Phases

We all go through the same financial phases in life, but we don't usually think about them until they're behind us. We may then look back and say, "Oh, we should have done something differently."

The **dependent stage** is when we're in our formative years as children. We go to school and try to find our place in the world. This stage is usually from early life until our early 20s. During that time, most of us depend on others for financial support.

We then graduate to the **accumulation stage**. That is when we hopefully find our way in life, build a career, raise a family, and accumulate assets. This stage is long, usually ranging from our 20s until right before retirement (often in our 60s).

If we're fortunate enough, we then move on to the **preservation stage**. That is where we find most of the families we help. It's the retirement phase of our lives, and a primary financial goal is to preserve assets for use in the present and near future.

Then we move to the **distribution stage**. That is when our assets are distributed to others, be it in the form of spending for expenses or leaving a financial legacy to loved ones.

It's important to understand that different tools are used for different purposes during each stage. What you might do in the accumulation phase may not always positively affect the distribution phase or other phases.

THE BIG 4

Financial Protection	**Tax Protection**
Nursing Home Protection	**Asset Protection**

With that understanding of life's financial phases, let's go back and dig deeper into the Big Four issues of estate planning. They include financial protection, nursing home protection, tax protection, and asset protection.

THE "BIG FOUR" ISSUES

Issue #1: Financial Protection

FINANCIAL PROTECTION

Accumulation vs. Preservation

Accumulation = Risky   **Preservation = Safe**

When you move from the accumulation phase to the preservation phase, you're the same, and your assets are the same. But the rules change. Protection becomes more important than in the past.

In the accumulation stage, you can accept greater levels of risk. However, once you're in the preservation phase, it's dangerous to absorb high levels of risk because the time horizon has shortened.

For example, in your 40s you can handle a financial catastrophe like a big market crash because you have time to recover. Yes, it's concerning, but you can shrug it off because you have plenty of time to earn it back. But if you're in your 70s and experience financial doom, you might panic because it could mean a big lifestyle change. You simply don't have the time to make it back up.

In the accumulation phase, you might invest in stocks, mutual funds, and options, which can all be risky, but they can also bring great rewards. In the preservation phase, it may be prudent to gravitate toward safer bets such as certificates of deposit (CDs), savings accounts, bonds, and Treasury bills. The growth potential with these assets isn't as great, but they are generally much safer and less volatile than the typical accumulation phase investments.

FINANCIAL PROTECTION

Accumulation vs. Preservation

Accumulation = Risky	**Preservation = Safe**
Stocks	Certificates of Deposit
Equities	Savings Accounts
Mutual Funds	Bonds
Options	Treasury Bills
Very Risky = High Growth	**Very Safe = Low Growth**

THE GOAL IN ESTATE PLANNING IS TO HAVE THE BEST OF BOTH WORLDS
* PLUS *

- Protection from Lawsuits, Nursing Homes, and Probate
- Being positioned for Income, Accumulation, Legacy or Death benefit
- Out Performing the S&P

SKOLNIK RETIREMENT SOLUTIONS

Estate planning aims to achieve the best of both worlds—growth and safety—while also addressing additional protections. Let's face it. Sometimes bad things happen to good people. So proper estate planning aims to protect from lawsuits, nursing home expenses, and probate. The key is to provide protection and growth without stifling the assets completely.

Those assets should be positioned for income, accumulation, legacy, or death benefit, depending on your specific situation. For example, we want to make sure your assets are safe but can still outperform the S&P 500. There are ways to do that; we just have to find the best way for you and your family.

So what is the holy grail of estate planning? It's the advantages of the accumulation stage, the safety of the preservation stage, comprehensive protection, and retirement income that can grow to potentially outpace inflation.

We strive to protect and preserve up to 100 percent of a family's assets.

Issue #2: Nursing Home Protection

The second issue that must be addressed is nursing home protection. This is another complex and misunderstood issue in estate planning.

Using our home state of Ohio as an example, the current median cost of home health care is about $45,000 a year. Assisted living is $47,000 annually, and full nursing home care is $77,000 per year. If you need Alzheimer's, memory, or dementia care, you have to add about 40 percent to those numbers.

In 2012, total spending (public, out-of-pocket and other private spending) for long-term care was $219.9 billion, or 9.3% of all U.S. personal health care spending. This is projected to increase to $346 billion in 2040. Source: The Family Care Givers Alliance 2015.[2]

To put that into perspective, let's do some math. Costs vary, but in our area, the monthly cost of nursing home care runs about $8,000 to $12,500 as of this writing. For the sake of ease, let's use $10,000 a month. For 12 months, that's $120,000 per year, most likely for the rest of your life. And if you have a spouse who also has to go into assisted living or a nursing facility, it could be financially devastating.

Liquidating your assets for end-of-life care is vastly avoidable. If there's a 70 percent chance of needing this care, you at least ought to understand how to offset the costs, mitigate them, or avoid them completely.

---

[2] *https://www.caregiver.org/resource/selected-long-term-care-statistics/ Viewed: Aug 2023*

HOW DO AVERAGE PEOPLE PROTECT THEMSELVES?

Long-Term Care Insurance	Veteran's Benefits
Medicare	Personal Savings

How do everyday people protect themselves from expensive long-term care? They rely on long-term care insurance, veterans benefits, Medicare, and personal savings.

The protections you have (or don't have) in place can significantly affect how you spend the later years of your life. We'll discuss that in much greater depth in Chapter Four.

Issue #3: Tax Protection

The third issue of our Big Four is taxation. In this country, we pay an endless list of taxes—income, property, gift, capital gains, sales, and so on. We're taxed literally to death and in some cases, even after death.

Your annual tax liability isn't of great concern here. What matters more for estate planning is the aggregate amount of money your estate is going to pay in taxes on your "stuff."

There is one tax that few people remember until it's too late, and that's the tax on inherited individual retirement accounts (IRAs). The rules have changed on inherited IRAs, particularly if they're left to anyone other than a spouse. And it's a big issue that affects virtually everyone. How much money are we talking about? According to the Investment Company Institute, "Collectively, Americans had more than $39 trillion in wealth earmarked for old age at the end of 2021."[3]

---

[3] *https://crsreports.congress.gov/product/pdf/IF/IF12117/2*

THE "BIG FOUR" ISSUES

THERE IS ONE TAX NOBODY IS TALKING ABOUT:

The Tax on Inherited IRAs

It is a Universal Issue. Seniors in the USA have $41 Trillion dollars in IRAs

$41,000,000,000,000

Elizabeth A. Myers, May, 2022

SKOLNIK RETIREMENT SOLUTIONS

Let's look at the history of IRAs. Introduced in 1974, they give Americans the privilege to put untaxed dollars aside for tax-deferred growth in a qualified account called a traditional IRA. Money you've earned and already paid taxes on can also be put in qualified accounts, but those are called Roth IRAs, and they follow different rules that we won't get into here.

Traditional IRAs are now meant for retirement. The original rules said you could access the money at age 59½, but if you withdrew before that, you'd have to pay taxes and penalties.

If you had money in a traditional IRA when you reached age 70½, the government required you to start taking required minimum distributions (RMDs). These are mandatory withdrawals designed to get you to start paying the taxes that were deferred while the IRAs grew. They're a way for the government to collect tax revenue.

THE TAX ON INHERITED IRAs

Prior to 2020
- You could not touch until you turned 59.5 (without penalty)
- When you turn 70.5 you had to take RMDs
- required minimum distributions
- The kids get the money tax amortized to the children's life expectancy

~88 years old = 30+ years

High but not crazy!

Under the old rules, when you passed away and your spouse was your named beneficiary, there was no inheritance cost or taxes, but the RMD requirement continued. When your spouse died (or if you didn't have a spouse), the IRA would go to the next named beneficiary, typically children or grandchildren. Historically, these beneficiaries were allowed to amortize the money over their respective life expectancies, which stretched out the tax payments.

This strategy was often called the "stretch IRA." If the beneficiaries were young and not yet in high tax brackets, the overall tax burden wasn't that bad.

THE TAX ON INHERITED IRAs

After 2020
- The Secure Act
- When you turn 70.5 you had to take RMDs
 RMDs raised to age 72
- Tax amortized to the children's life expectancy ~88 years old
 Now only amortized for 10 years!

But all that changed with the Setting Every Community Up for Retirement Enhancement Act (SECURE Act) in 2020, and then again in 2022 with the SECURE Act 2.0. There were many small changes, but two are significant. First, the age for RMDs was raised to 72, then to 73, and in 2033 it will be 75). Second, your heirs can no longer amortize the taxes on your traditional IRAs over their life expectancies. Instead, IRAs now have to be amortized over 10 years.

So politicians did what they do best. They raised taxes without explicitly raising taxes. Instead, they changed the rules of how the money is collected. It's now basically three times the tax in one-third the time.

A common scenario we've seen is someone inheriting an IRA in their 50s and living into their 80s. That's 30 years. But now the window is only 10 years. That may be a wonderful decision for federal tax collectors, but it's absolutely terrible for the $41 trillion in inherited IRAs.

Thankfully, good estate planning can greatly reduce or even eliminate this issue. However, people don't understand these options because they don't consider estate planning in broad terms that encompass everything (now and in the future).

Issue #4: Asset Protection

As a reminder, we said our mission was threefold with different levels of complexity.

The first objective is to help preserve and protect assets from lawsuits. For example, we mentioned Mark's case where his assets were consumed by the liabilities stemming from a car accident he caused. Another asset drain is probate, which is simple to avoid by planning ahead of time. A third retirement time bomb is nursing home costs, which is a complicated topic we will discussed in great detail in Chapter Four.

The fourth part is asset protection against market fluctuations. Remember, with time on your side, big drops in asset values can be weathered. But as you age, there is less time for recovery. That's why a different mix of assets is a prudent course. In other words, you must adjust. Otherwise, a market crash could be devastating.

These are the Big Four issues in estate planning. And we can help you with them.

OUR MISSION

1. Preserve and Protect Assets from:

- Lawsuits
- Probate Court
- Nursing Home Costs
- Market Fluctuations

2. Simplify and Consolidate your stuff

3. Maximize and Multiply then distribute your assets when you are done with them in a way that is:

- Simple
- Easy
- And in a Tax-advantaged manor

SKOLNIK RETIREMENT SOLUTIONS

Again, our mission is threefold. We aim to preserve and protect your assets. We then want to simplify and consolidate your "stuff" so you can control and dictate your world for as long as possible. Finally, we seek to maximize, multiply, and distribute your assets. This helps ensure that your accumulated nest egg is distributed precisely to who you want in a simple, easy, and tax-advantaged manner.

Chapter Three

LEGAL PLANNING (OR HOW MOST PEOPLE SEE ESTATE PLANNING)

As we look at legal planning, let's start with this important disclosure. We are not attorneys. But when it comes to estate planning, the right kind of attorney is critical because there are five essential legal documents that everybody absolutely needs.

It doesn't matter what size estate you have. Whether you have $50 or $5 million, you need these documents.

THE FIVE ESSENTIAL DOCUMENTS

Legal Documents
- Last Will & Testament
- General Power of Attorney
- Health Care Power of Attorney
- Living Will
- General/Universal HIPPA Release

The last will and testament is vitally important. It's so important that our home state of Ohio will give you a free one if you don't have one. But in such cases, you get what you pay for (and you probably won't like the asset distribution).

In Ohio, if you don't have a will or an extensive estate plan to protect you, one-third of your money will go to your spouse, while the remaining two-thirds will go to all of your kids. That's not necessarily fair to your spouse, is it? But that's the law in Ohio (as of this writing).

That's why we often say, "Either you have a plan or you're part of somebody else's plan." You definitely don't want to be part of somebody else's plan, especially if it's the state of Ohio (or any other state for that matter).

The general power of attorney and the health care power of attorney are important as well and can be looked at together (they're often combined and called a durable power of attorney). The rules for this document have become quite specialized, so you need to be sure you're knowledgeable about them and update your documents accordingly. Some people call these the "helping documents" because they provide a voice to the voiceless.

One of our family stories is a good illustration of this concept. Skip's father-in-law (Libby's grandfather) passed away years ago. When he went to the hospital, he could not make decisions for himself. If he hadn't had power of attorney documents in place, someone—likely a family member or friend—would have had to go to court to get guardianship to be able to make decisions on his behalf. If you're like our family, you probably don't want courts involved in your health and financial decisions. That's why these documents are essential.

Sometimes the documents are helpful in other ways. For example, one family we work with spends part of the winter in Florida. While they were there, a storm blew a tree over on their home. It hit the side of the house and caused damage that had to be fixed right away.

The last thing this family wanted was to fly home to get the money to fix a gutter and a window. So the son, who has power of attorney, went to the bank, showed his identification, and said, "I need $5,000 to fix my mom and dad's house; here are the documents." The banker had no choice but to comply, so the son got the money needed for repairs, and the situation was resolved.

A living will tells people what you want to be done (or not done) with your body at the end of life when you cannot speak for yourself. For example, do you want to be kept alive by heroic measures? Do you want to live in a vegetative state? Do you want supplemental respiration, hydration, and food withheld or provided?

Those are decisions best made by you, together with your spouse, when you're in good health and rooted firmly in your beliefs. Don't leave the proverbial "pull-the-plug" decision to anybody. Put your wishes in writing, keep them updated, and make sure they'll stand up to any conflicting requests.

A general or universal medical privacy release gives specifically designated people all the information needed to make intelligent medical decisions. If you've been to a doctor in the last 10 years, you've heard of the Health Information Portability and Accountability Act (HIPAA). A power of attorney for health care gives someone the ability to make decisions for you if you can't. The HIPAA release gives them access to important information so they're informed when making those decisions.

Most times when you go to the doctor, you sign a HIPAA release that's usually temporary. Let's say you need a tooth extracted. Before the procedure, you would sign a release that says if something goes wrong, your family members or anybody else you name can make decisions for you if you're unable to make them yourself. And that's great.

But here's where HIPAA is not helpful. Let's say you're driving home and get in a car crash. You're badly injured and rushed to the hospital. The doctors in the emergency room call your family and say there are three options to bring you back to health. Your family would have to choose, but without a general or universal HIPAA release, they wouldn't have access to important information to inform the decision. Still, they'd have to tell the doctors what to do.

While that might seem wrong, that's the world we live in. No one will accommodate you by breaking the rules. So you must have all these documents in place in advance.

Probate: What It Is, Why It's a Problem, and How to Avoid It

All five of the documents we just mentioned have critical implications for your legal planning. But there's another issue that deserves a special place in this discussion. The issue is probate.

We've said that you need a will, and that's true. But even if you have a will, it can create another problem. It guarantees your family will go to probate court.

That may not be the case when everything passes from one spouse to the other. But when someone dies—will or no will—the probate court is involved unless assets are transferred by some other transfer method. That can affect bank accounts, real estate, personal property, and any business interests.

WHAT IS PROBATE AND WHY DO WE NEED IT:

- Governs everything in your Last Will & Testament
- A Court determines the outcome of the distribution of your assets
- Probates Role:
  - Find the Money
  - Pay the Bills
  - Do what the Will said...

Most people don't understand what probate does. It's not there to protect you, your stuff, your money, your kids, your house, and so on. It's there to protect the people you might (or might not) owe money to. Specifically, it governs everything in your will. In theory, that's good. It causes time to stop and ensures everything is done correctly.

LEGAL PLANNING (OR HOW MOST PEOPLE SEE ESTATE PLANNING)

The court can do whatever it wants to determine the outcome of the distribution. To understand this better, let's break it down into the probate court's three specific roles.

The first is to find all the money. When someone passes away, the court calls a time-out and looks at everything with a title, deed, and anything where a designated beneficiary should have been named.

The second role is to pay all the legitimate bills. That occurs before any distributions to family members or charities.

The third role is to do what the will says. Your will simply directs the probate court on what you want to be done with your estate.

WHY PROBATE IS AN ISSUE

- Expensive
  - Attorneys to charge 8-12%
  - Think 10% - $400,000 estate cost $40,000

Probate court has its three specific roles, but there are also three major problems with probate.

First, it's expensive. In Ohio, attorneys can charge 8–12 percent of the estate for their probate services. So how much do they really charge? The highest percentage, of course. For an estate with $400,000 in assets, that's $48,000. That hefty fee is probably why many attorneys don't seem to want to avoid probate. They make a lot of money going to court. But we believe that money should go to your family, not an attorney.

WHY PROBATE IS AN ISSUE

- Lengthy
  - The average Probate Takes 18.5 Months

Next, probate can be a lengthy process. If you start a probate court case today in Ohio, it won't be handled for four months. That's because everybody gets a chance to make a claim against your estate. Who can make a claim? Anybody you owe money to can make a claim. Whether it's the credit card bill, the gas bill, taxes, the funeral home, doctors, or anyone else, they can file a claim against the estate. And if the claim is legitimate and legal, they will be paid. Right now, the entire process in Ohio averages almost 19 months.

WHY PROBATE IS AN ISSUE

- Public
  - US Sunshine Laws
  - All documents are viewable on the internet

The third problem is that the process is a matter of public record. It's all visible to anyone who wants to see it. Most people don't think about this aspect of probate, but it can be devastating to the surviving family. Let's say a relative of yours passes away. Thanks to US sunshine laws, anyone can go to your relative's county and pull up the probate records. It's all viewable either online or at the courthouse.

Anyone can find out precisely what the deceased owned, who they owed, and where every penny went. They can also see if any family members were left out of the will. It's all public. Most of the families we help don't like that, which is completely understandable.

Let's recap the probate court. It's expensive— up to 12% of the estate in Ohio. It's lengthy—the average is 18.5 months in Ohio, but we've seen the process go on for years. And it's public—anyone can look at everything. All that is just to give your kids your stuff.

Here's the most important aspect of probate court: it's completely avoidable. So many people go to probate and don't realize it's a problem until it's too late. If they knew, they'd probably do what's needed to skip probate altogether. Trust us; it's a miserable process.

LEGAL PLANNING (OR HOW MOST PEOPLE SEE ESTATE PLANNING)

For years we focused our work almost exclusively on avoiding probate and all the bad stuff we just mentioned. But the world of estate planning has changed.

One thing that's changed is the cost of long-term medical insurance. Probate court is a big deal, costing 10–12 percent of your estate value in Ohio. But as mentioned, long-term care can cost you up to $120,000 a year. So probate has become a molehill compared to the mountain that is nursing home costs.

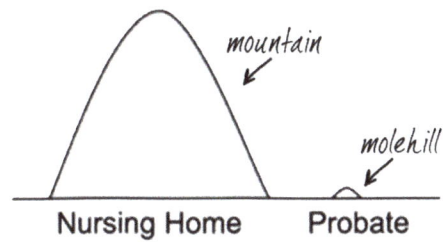

$120,000

Sometimes people forget about the probate molehill. Or they focus on the molehill and forget about the mountain—nursing home costs. It's not just $120,000. It's $120,000 per year, possibly for the rest of your life.

From our perspective, probate becomes irrelevant as we help people with the bigger problem of nursing home protection. As you'll see in the next chapter, a comprehensive estate plan that provides nursing home protection eliminates a lot of potential problems.

Chapter Four

OUR PROCESS FOR NURSING HOME PROTECTION

If you become one of the 70 percent of Americans who need nursing home care, how prepared are you to pay for it?

Your Financial Resources

If you or your spouse needs to spend some time in a nursing home beyond simple rehab for a replaced hip or knee, you could find yourself making a list of all your financial resources to help pay for it. That would include personal savings, pensions, IRAs, home equity loans, reverse mortgages, marketable whole life insurance policies, long-forgotten savings bonds, and maybe more.

Does that sound daunting? It certainly can be. But if you or someone you love needs nursing care, there are three other options to consider.

MAJOR CONCERN: LONG-TERM CARE EXPENSE

Financial Resources
- Medicare
- Long-Term Care Insurance
- Veteran's Benefits

SKOLNIK RETIREMENT SOLUTIONS

Long-Term Care Insurance

Historically, long-term care insurance was a way to offset or mitigate the high cost of nursing homes, but that's not the case anymore. Today, every one of our clients wants to discuss long-term care insurance either because they bought it and regret it or because they didn't buy it and regret it. And if they're thinking of buying it now, it's too expensive. The problem in all these scenarios is the cost involved.

About a decade ago, we used a lot of long-term care insurance in our planning. Nearly three dozen companies offered good long-term care insurance coverage back then. But the cost of long-term care has since skyrocketed. As a result, today there are not nearly as many insurers offering these policies.

Why? Because they can no longer afford it. They're going out of business. The solution for these insurers was to go to regulators and beg for help because they couldn't make money on these policies.

LONG-TERM CARE INSURANCE

- Cost $1,700 - $3,500 per person per year
- Approximately 50% greater if 70 years old or over
- Daily benefit of $100 - $200 per day (80% of policies)
- 0 to 4 years benefit period (70% of policies)

And the regulators let them change the contracts. First, they let them change the rates without clients knowing it. Now, each new yearly statement brings a new rate that you either pay or you don't. And if you don't, the insurer's responsibility to you ends. Then, depending on your particular contract, all the premiums you paid over the years could be lost. Yearly premiums on these policies went from $1,700 to $3,500. And if you're more than 70 years old, it could be even more. Thus, coverage became cost-prohibitive.

Next, insurers put daily maximums on benefits. Today, about 80 percent of policies have benefit maximums of $100 to $200 per day. That's roughly $36,500–$73,000 per year. As we know from the last chapter, that's not enough money on average to adequately cover nursing home costs.

Insurers also lengthened the elimination period, which is how long you have to live in a facility before you can make claims against your long-term care insurance. Initially, it was 60 days. That increased to 90 and then to 120. We even recently saw 180 days. What is the insurance company doing during those 180 days? Frankly, it's waiting for you to die—gruesome but true.

Finally, insurers added a benefit period. Most policies today are only good for four years of coverage. When you throw in the elimination period, it's actually three and a half years because of the potential 180-day wait for the policy to kick in.

All in all, long-term care insurance policies have been gutted. They're now prohibitively expensive and offer increasingly limited coverage.

LONG-TERM CARE INSURANCE

Do the Math:
The average policy today covers $197 per day
The average long-term care facility costs $10,000 per month
Divided by 30 days = $333 per day
$333 - $197 = $136 per day x 365 days =

$49,640.00 SHORT EACH YEAR

It might help to look at an actual example to see what a current long-term care insurance deal looks like. A client came in and said, "I'm prepared. I'm not worried about long-term care. I have insurance." We replied, "Great! Let's check the policy details."

It turns out that her policy was average at best. It covered $197 per day after 180 days. But the average long-term care facility costs $10,000 per month, or roughly $333 per day. That left her short $136 per day.

That shortfall is about $50,000 per year. When we pointed that out, she said she couldn't afford $50,000 per year for a nursing home stay. So she didn't have the peace of mind she thought she had. Instead, she really had a false sense of security.

Do we still use long-term care insurance? Rarely. The whole idea behind insurance is pooling or sharing the risk. But when it comes to long-term care, we'd rather avoid sharing the risk of a pool. We want to avoid this risk altogether, and we'll show you soon exactly how to do that.

Veterans Benefits

Whether it's for a veteran or a veteran's spouse, there is a program we love. It's called the Aid and Attendance benefit. Not enough veterans have heard of it, especially those who can benefit from it. This benefit is a big federal program administered through the Department of Veterans Affairs (VA). Let's break it down.

VETERAN BENEFITS

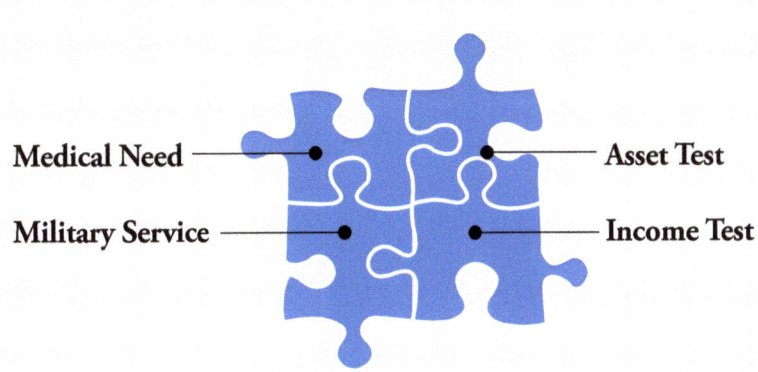

The pieces for this program fit together like a puzzle. The first component is **military service**. To be eligible, you must have served at least 90 consecutive days, including at least one day during World War II, the Korean War, the Vietnam War, or the Gulf War.

The next is the **asset** test. The thinking here is that if you have too much money, you don't need the veterans benefits. Through November 2023, the net worth limit to be eligible for VA pension benefits such as the Aid and Attendance benefit is $150,538 of assets and income for a veteran and a spouse. Unlike Medicare or Medicaid, which both have a five-year, look-back period, this VA program at the moment does not have such a requirement.

What's a look-back period? When you're applying for a benefit, a look-back period is how far into the past your financial transactions can be reviewed to see if you've moved any assets in order to qualify. For example, in the case of the VA, let's assume you're denied because you have too many assets. Without a look-back period, you can reposition your assets in the coming days and then reapply and be approved.

The five-year, look-back period applied to Medicare and Medicaid is why many people are unprepared for nursing home costs. By the time they realize they have the problem of too many assets, it's too late to fix what they needed to fix five years ago. But for veterans benefits, that's not the case today.

The next two pieces are **medical need** and an **income test**. These are combined because what counts is the ratio of the two, not the absolute amount. If your medical need is beyond a particular ratio and you've met the other two requirements (military service and the asset test), your income doesn't matter, and these funds are available to you. They're not only available to you but also to your surviving spouse. If you're a veteran and you pass away, your surviving spouse can still get these benefits.

What are the benefits? These figures are for 2023. Starting at the bottom, a surviving spouse gets $1,100–$1,200 per month. A single veteran gets $1,700–$1,800 per month. A veteran with dependents and/or a spouse starts at around $2,100 per month. Two veterans in a household, which happens more often than you think, get nearly $35,000 of tax-free money each year for the rest of their lives.[4] It's a good program and a good way to offset or mitigate long-term care costs.

MEDICARE YOUR FIRST LINE OF FINANCIAL DEFENSE

---

[4] *https://americanveteransaid.com/landing/lp_2/NEW/aid_and_attendance_2.html Viewed: Aug 2023*

Medicare

Most people don't think of Medicare when they're doing estate planning. But it's crucial because Medicare is your first line of financial defense.

4 PARTS OF MEDICARE

PART A	PART B	PART C	PART D
Hospital Insurance	Medical Insurance	Medicare Advantage Plans	Prescription Drug Plans

There are these four parts to Medicare: Parts A, B, C, and D. Part A is hospital insurance. If something happens to you and you need to be admitted to a hospital, hopefully this coverage helps get you back to normal. Part B is medical insurance, which is preventive care (hopefully it keeps you from needing Part A). Part C is also known as Medicare Advantage (an alternative to Part A and Part B that's offered through private insurers). Part D is for prescription drugs.

PART A: YOUR FIRST DEFENSE!

Hospital Insurance

- Hospital & Skilled nursing care
- Hospice
- Semi-private rooms
- It does not cover:
  - Long-Term Care
  - Custodial Care

Medicare Part A is truly your first line of defense. If you get ill or something happens and you are rushed to the hospital, Part A covers you first. It pays for hospital costs, skilled nursing services, short-term care, and hospice. With Part A you get a semi-private room, which means you'll have a roommate. But you must know that Part A does not cover long-term care or custodial care. It's a short-term Band-Aid at best.

Let's look at the dollars. Keep in mind that they can change every year. In 2023, for days one through 20, you pay nearly nothing. There's an occasional test or related fee, but the vast majority is completely covered. For days 21 through 100, you pay $160 per day. After 100 days, get out your checkbook. Medicare Part A pays for 90 days of treatment every benefit period. If your hospital stay goes beyond all those days, you pay for all costs out of your own pocket.

These costs may seem mind boggling. Still, Medicare Part A remains your first line of financial defense for nursing home protection.

PART A: YOUR FIRST DEFENSE!

Hospital Insurance

What does it actually cover:
- Day 1-20 = You pay nothing
- Day 21-100 = You pay ~$160 p/day
- Day 100+ = You pay 100% Out of Pocket

You might think very few people spend three months in a hospital. You're right. It doesn't take long for someone at the hospital to suggest that you'd be better served at a step-down or rehabilitative facility. By the way, those are long-term care facilities. The reason the hospital does that is because eventually they have to start hunting down and collecting money from people who now owe $400 per day (or more). They would rather get the money from the government (i.e., Medicare) because it's easier.

The fact is that there is a lot of money involved with a long hospital stay. So it's essential to understand precisely how the system works.

The Major Concern with Long-Term Care Expenses after 90 Days

Long-term care expenses are a huge concern for older Americans, which is why we help so many people protect against nursing home costs. We described three main ways most people offset these costs—long-term care insurance, veterans benefits, and Medicare. But there's more to the story.

If you're not covered by long-term care insurance or veterans benefits, you're counting on Medicare. And we know how costs can escalate quickly. After 90 days, one of the first things that happens is a review of the last five years of your finances. You must present all your financial documents—every bank statement, savings account statement, land transfer—essentially everything you've done financially for the last five years. Administrators will scrutinize all of it carefully.

After that, you'll be asked a bunch of questions. All of it boils down to figuring out how you'll pay for your care.

The look-back review isn't an all-or-nothing calculation. For example, if it hasn't been a full five years since you repositioned assets, you don't lose all the benefits. It's a graduated process, which means each year counts as one-fifth of the five years (or 20 percent).

After one year, 20 percent is protected. After two years, it's 40 percent, and so on. If you go into a nursing home three years after repositioning assets, 60 percent of your assets cannot be "attached." However, in that case, you will want to do some crisis management. In our experience, out of the vulnerable 40 percent of assets, we can generally save about 65 percent of them.

Doing some quick math, you can protect about 80–85 percent of your assets in just three years. It's obviously better to wait the full five years. But that's not always possible. Options exist for shorter periods, and every year brings more options.

Protecting against the Look-Back Period

Admittedly, it's hard to understand how to answer something if you don't know the definition of the terms in the questions. So we're going to break down the concepts and provide some basic definitions. We're about to enter into the Medicaid world. Then we'll give you a framework of how this system actually works.

Earlier in the book we said, "Either you have a plan or you're part of someone else's plan." If you don't have a plan, there is one already there for you—long-term Medicaid. It varies by state, but we'll explain generally how it works and how much you might pay.

BASIC MEDICAID TERMS

- CSRA: Community Spouse Resource Allowance
- PRA: Patient Resource Allowance

Let's first cover some basic Medicaid definitions. Two important terms are the "community spouse resource allowance" (CSRA) and the "patient resource allowance" (PRA). Let's assume you are the patient and you're going into a nursing facility. Your spouse is staying home. The CSRA is the amount of money your spouse can keep. The PRA is the amount of money you're legally allowed to keep.

BASIC MEDICAID TERMS

- Countable Resource
- Exempt Resource

The next two items to explain are "countable resources" and "exempt resources." Countable resources are the assets included in the equation to figure out how much money you're going to pay for the rest of your life. In general, these are liquid assets such as cash, CDs, and so on. We love exempt resources because they're assets entirely left out of the equation. An example is your primary residence.

Now let's look at the "concept of the half loaf." Few people have heard of this concept, but it's the centerpiece of many nursing home plans. Nobody understands this until they're going through it, and then it's one of the most painful things they've ever done from a financial standpoint.

How the Half Loaf Works

Let's say your loaf is all the assets owned by you and your spouse. In most states, Medicaid breaks your loaf into two halves—the patient's half and the community spouse's half.

Let's say the whole loaf is worth $100,000. Medicaid is going to break it in half and put $50,000 in each pile. If you're the patient, $50,000 goes into your pile, and $50,000 goes into your spouse's pile. Now we'll encounter a concept you've probably heard of—the spend-down process.

Medicaid requires you to spend down your half of the loaf until it gets to your PRA. Right now, that's just $2,000.

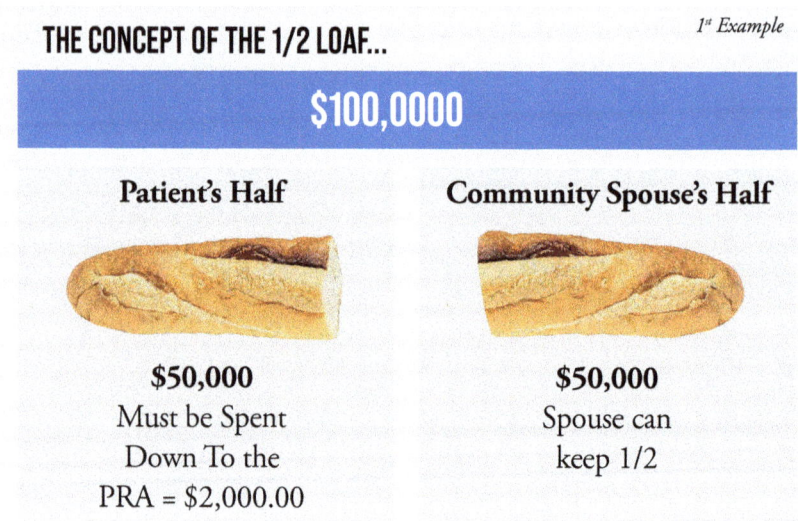

Now say the entire loaf is worth $200,000, so $100,000 is yours and $100,000 belongs to your spouse. Your spouse gets to keep half. But you have to spend down $98,000 to get to your $2,000 PRA.

What do you spend that on?

Some of the families we've helped needed an enormous TV because they can't see or hear well. That's acceptable. They also needed a lift chair, which of course is acceptable to help with mobility. It's a good thing your spouse can still keep half of everything—so far anyway.

Now let's say the whole loaf is worth $400,000, so $200,000 each. In the previous examples, you almost certainly didn't want to spend your half loaf down to $2,000. Well, now you have to spend $198,000 to reach the $2,000 PRA.

At least your spouse gets to keep half, right? No. This is where it gets terrible. Your spouse can keep half of everything, but only up to a maximum amount. And this amount changes regularly. Currently it's $148,620.

3rd Example

THE CONCEPT OF THE 1/2 LOAF...

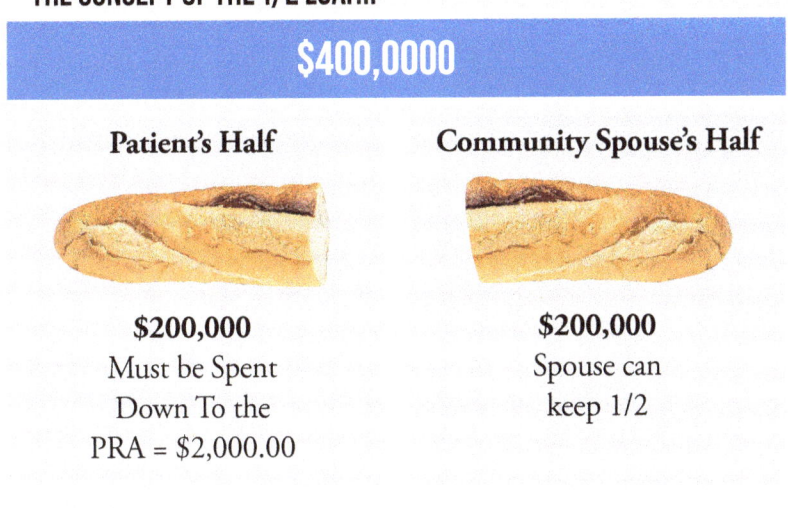

$400,0000

Patient's Half   **Community Spouse's Half**

$200,000
Must be Spent
Down To the
PRA = $2,000.00

$200,000
Spouse can
keep 1/2

THINK ABOUT THAT... $400,000 ESTATE NOW ONLY WORTH $128,000

Suddenly that loaf of bread is reduced to breadcrumbs. The $400,000 is down to just $139,400. That's your $2,000 PRA and the capped amount of $148,620 for your spouse.

It doesn't matter how much money you have. If you're on Medicaid, you're subject to this painful system. Once you reach the asset thresholds, then all the state and federal programs come in and take care of you for the rest of your life.

That's your plan unless you have a way to offset or mitigate these long-term care costs. But there's help. It's what we do every day. You can trust us that with proper estate planning, these kinds of spending requirements are avoidable.

The Nursing Home Example with No Preplanning

MEDICAID EXAMPLE WITH NO PLANNING

- Home (subject to Estate Recovery)
- $2,000 in assets
- One Car
- Personal Items (clothing, jewelry, etc.)
- Household Items (furniture, appliances, etc.)
- Funeral/Burial Contract(s)
- $1,500 Cash Surrender Value of Life Insurance
- Spouse: 50% up to a Max of $148,620

The Medicare and Medicaid programs look at all your assets. Here's a breakdown of how that works.

One asset is your income. Medicaid will not leave the community spouse destitute. It may take a lot but not everything. In general, the program looks at your home and your assets. The assets are split in the half-loaf spend-down process.

As for your home, by law the surviving spouse cannot be kicked out of the family home. Yes, Medicaid will take a portion of the assets. But once you get to the threshold of $2,000 for your PRA and $148,620 for your spouse's CSRA, no more money can be taken.

Instead, administrators keep track of everything they've spent on you, the patient. Then when your community spouse is done with the property, the state takes what's called the "first position." In essence, it takes the proceeds from a property sale.

When you hear of people who have lost their home and all their money to the nursing home, this is the process. It's called "estate recovery." And in our experience, the state of Ohio is incredibly aggressive with it.

So your home is subject to estate recovery. And you're allowed to keep $2,000 as the patient. In addition, the family is allowed to keep just one vehicle.

Next are your personal items and household items, which are usually lumped together. The state doesn't care about your cuckoo clock, jewelry, or appliances. It also doesn't care about the gold bars you've been hiding in your basement as long as you purchased them more than five years ago. The asset look-back is done to keep people from hiding assets. To receive long-term Medicaid benefits, you can't reposition assets unless you did it at least five years ago.

Another part of the asset review is funeral and burial contracts. Not only is a preplanned funeral crucial to a comprehensive estate plan, but it can also be used for crisis management, which we'll describe in a moment.

Then there's life insurance. If there's a cash value to it, you lose it. We'll cover life insurance in more detail in a bit.

Finally, there's the 50 percent of assets your spouse can keep. Remember, the cap on that is $148,620.

In a nutshell, that's how your estate works with no planning. You probably don't like what you just read. Make no mistake, we don't either. That's why we do two types of advanced planning.

Look ahead five, 10, 15, or 20 years, and position assets to suit your needs. This method helps you find the greatest solutions for your family and moves things around accordingly.

The second approach is more like crisis management. It's when someone is going into a nursing home within the next 12 months (sometimes within one month). In these circumstances, we need to work around the look-back period and find the least-worst options. Frankly, that's because then the possibilities are terrible. This is a stop-gap approach that results from years of not planning. We can help do some things, but it's certainly not an ideal scenario.

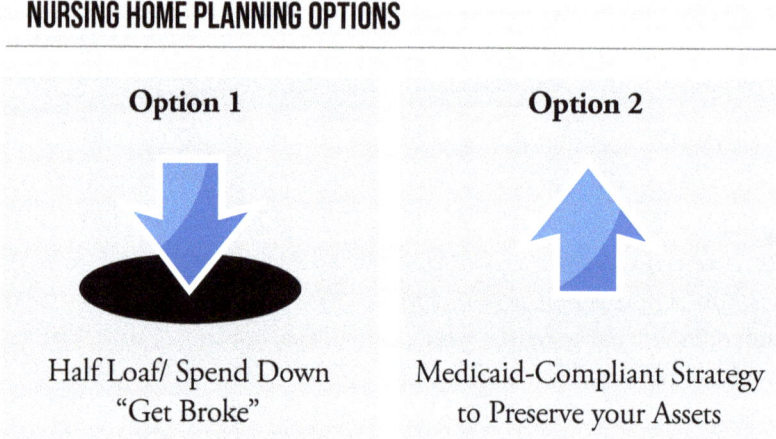

Nursing home protection can be effectively boiled down to two options. The first is the half-loaf spend-down process where you have to spend it all, and then the government will take care of you for the rest of your life. It's an option, but not one most families would choose if they knew better.

The second option is the one we like much better—Medicaid-compliant strategies to preserve and protect your assets. For emphasis, let's repeat that phrase—Medicaid-compliant. These are Medicaid's rules. Our strategies comply with them.

To be clear, this is not a matter of hiding assets. Instead, it's about repositioning assets according to the rules that Medicaid sets out. We show Medicaid exactly what we do, and it works well for our clients.

You can do this for yourself too. However, Medicare-Medicaid information that explains the process is lengthy and complicated.

Our goal is to put you in the situation where you're prepared for the conversation with nursing home administrators about your last five years of financial activity. When they ask, "What do you have and how are you going to pay for this?" you'll answer, "I've got $400,000 in assets, but according to your rules, you can't attach them."

This is what it's like to plan ahead and be prepared. It's advanced, master-class-level planning. And if you're retired (or nearing it), you need to understand this.

THE AVERAGE AMERICAN STICKS THEIR HEAD IN THE SAND... UNTIL IT IS TOO LATE!

70% of people now age 65 and older will need some period of extended care during the remainder of their life.

U.S. news and World Report, November 2018

Too many people take the "ostrich approach" of sticking their heads in the sand until it's too late. Remember, 70 percent of people ages 65 and older need some period of extended care. How you'll pay for it is not something you want to leave unplanned.

CLIENT EXAMPLE: MIKE & BRENDA

Mike was a marketing professional
$0 pension + Social Security

Brenda was a Teacher with a $4,400 p/m Pension + Health Care coverage

Health Issues:

$300,000 in combined assets

- $126,0000* = $174,000 at Risk

By Utilizing our knowledge and expertise we were able to protect:

- $110,000 of assets
- Mikes Full Social Security
- 42% of Brenda's Monthly Income for Mike
- Full Health coverage for Mike

We also repositioned the $126,000 to protect it from the Nursing home and Ultimately go directly to their kids

78.6% Mike and Brenda saved 78.5% of the family assets.

SKOLNIK RETIREMENT SOLUTIONS

* 126,000 was the CSRA @ 2022

Chapter Five

OUR PROCESS FOR PROTECTING ASSETS

When we sit down with your family, we start by getting to know you. That means understanding your goals and wishes for the future. In short, we need to learn how we can best help you.

Step #1: Learn about You

We first learn about you and all your "stuff," or what you have and what's important to you. We discuss your goals and motivations. That could include family wishes, charitable desires, and so on. We want to make sure that all those main objectives are points of focus for your estate plan. Then we lay our OctaView Retirement System™ over what we've identified and examine it through various lenses.

How do we protect assets? How do we make sure income is still good, no matter the circumstances? For example, when covering two spouses, we want to ensure the surviving spouse has the income to live the lifestyle they want. If not, we make adjustments.

OCTAVIEW RETIREMENT SYSTEM™

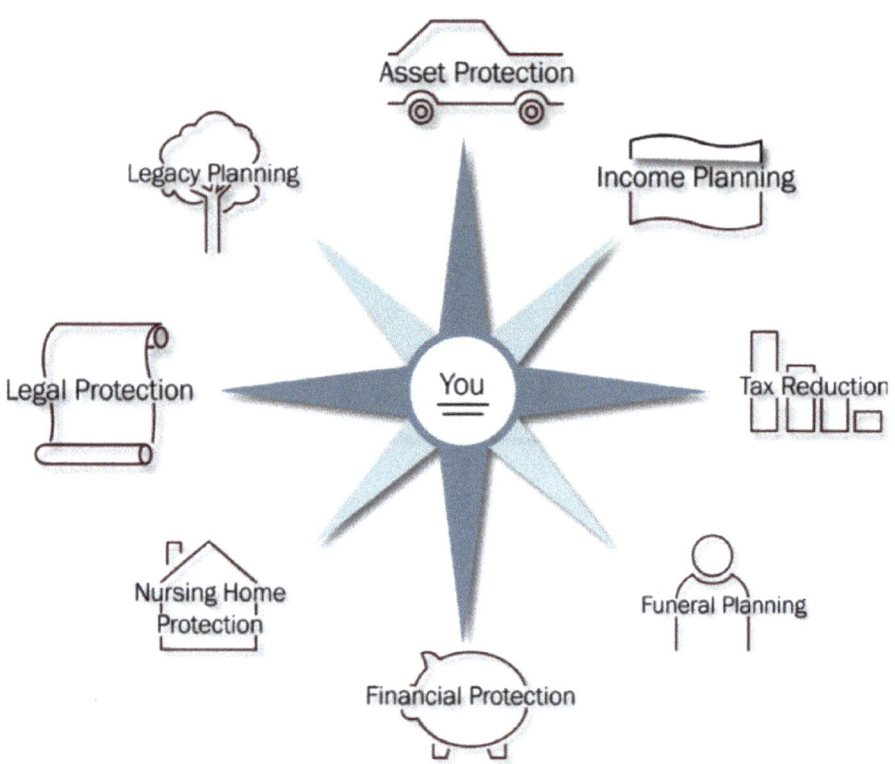

We also seek to reduce tax burdens wherever possible. That includes annual taxes but more importantly focuses on your tax burden in relation to your long-term care needs. We also factor in what we think is happening with local, state, and federal taxes (we believe there are changes ahead).

Next comes funeral planning. There's a 100 percent chance that you will pass away at some point, so why not be prepared? Our goal is that when the time comes, the surviving spouse needs to make one phone call and two decisions. The phone call is to the funeral home. The two decisions are what day and what time the service will be held. Everything else is handled, eliminating the need for debate or discussion. In short, you've prepared for how you want things handled.

In situations of loss, not being organized only adds to the pain. We've helped families sort through decades-old financial statements looking for life insurance policies. In one case, a family had always been told the policies were in place. But when they needed them, they couldn't find any records. When we found them, the policy death benefits totaled $85,000.

We strongly advocate creating a "When I Die" file. It should have updated statements for all accounts, insurance policies, trust and legal documents, and as a more recent addition, all online account passwords.

Then we look at financial protection, nursing home protection, legal protection, and your desired legacy. Some people have particular goals for their heirs—kids, grandkids, cousins, nieces, or nephews—and we help position assets to achieve those goals.

Again, we look at the Big Four, specifically:

- Financial Protection
- Nursing Home Protection
- Tax Protection
- Asset Protection

Step #2: Determine a Legal Entity

After we examine your situation through all those lenses, we work with attorneys to determine what kind of protective legal entity would work best for your situation. Sometimes we use limited liability companies (LLCs), S corporations, C corporations, or closely held family partnerships.

We only look into the realm of trusts if needed. Ohio has many possible trust arrangements (we use nine, depending on the situation). Some are revocable, while others are irrevocable. The right one depends entirely on your needs.

Ultimately, we want to make sure there's a unique legal entity protecting your family. Why an entity? Remember, our goal is to preserve and protect your assets from lawsuits. Having your "stuff" owned by a legal entity protects you and your loved ones from personal liabilities.

The same holds true for probate. You don't go to probate if you don't own anything. It's also true for the nursing home. If you don't own anything, nothing gets "attached," so you can go to the nursing home without selling large portions of your estate (assuming you're prepared for the five-year look-back).

That said, we make sure you maintain control. We want you to be able to buy or sell things, take income, take principal, change beneficiaries, change trustees, or whatever else you may see fit.

We also make sure important legal documents are in place. They include a will, a power of attorney for health care, a power of attorney for business affairs, a living will, and a HIPAA release. That is all done within that legal entity.

Step #3: Fund the Entity

In the third step, we fund your family's legal entity, whatever form it takes. Anything not owned by the entity is at risk. All too often, people tell us they have an LLC, a trust, or something else. They think they're protected. But when we ask what's owned by their LLC or trust, we often get blank, questioning looks in response.

These corporate/trust documents are often beautiful. But they only protect what they own. That ownership function is why we fund the entity.

We learn about everything you own in order to understand the full picture and how we can protect assets, whether inside or outside the entity. We then position your assets as needed. Of course, not everything can be handled that way, so we need to be sure there are no negative repercussions as you make decisions.

Life insurance falls into this analysis too. We have to "preposition" life insurance policies. Let's say you have $300,000 of life insurance coverage. You've worked with us for seven years, and everything is in place. When you pass, the insurance money goes to your spouse. But if your spouse needs to go into a nursing home, there's a brand new five-year look-back review. So life insurance policies need to be protected along with everything else. That is what our team does.

It all comes down to some key questions. Who do you want to be like? Do you want to be like Mark who was completely unprepared? Would you rather be like Bob and Jean who thought they were prepared but weren't and only left $9,000 for each kid? Or do you want to be like Brenda and Mike who were fully prepared because they had a comprehensive plan for everything?

Our goal, just like with Brenda and Mike, is to make sure that when something unfortunate happens in life, as it inevitably will, you have options. Having options is always better than having something forced on you. That is especially true in a crisis situation.

Planning early is ideal, but it's never too late to start planning. For most people, the best time to start was many years ago. But it's fine if that didn't happen. The next best time is today.

You've worked a lifetime to build your net worth. It doesn't matter if it's a few bucks or a mountain of money; we're happy to work with you. If you have $5 million and need $400,000 to get the care needed for the rest of your life, you have room for error. We help families like that. But if your entire estate is $300,000–$500,000 and it will cost you $300,000–$500,000 for your care, mistakes can be financially devastating. There's no room for error. We help families in this area too.

The majority of our clients are average American families. They're independent business owners, automotive workers, civil servants, and firefighters. They're not rich, but they have money set aside, and they're certainly not poor. Regardless of your family's dollar amount, you worked a lifetime to accumulate it, and it needs to be protected.

Ideally, estate planning should be something you enjoy doing because you understand it and are building a plan for your life that reflects your wishes and goals. You've worked a lifetime to amass what you have. Protecting it should be something you look forward to like your favorite hobby.

Chapter Six

LIFE'S CLOSING CHAPTER

One of the most difficult topics to discuss is funeral plans. That's a bit odd since we're all going to be there someday. No one is getting out alive. But cultural taboos make it problematic in our society to talk about death.

Yet funeral preplanning is a key step in estate plan readiness. And it's incredibly important to have a default plan in place during a time of grief.

As mentioned, we strive to have our clients in a position of "one call, two choices" for funerals. That means there's one call to the funeral home of choice and two funeral-related decisions to make—date and time. Everything else is already in place. In fact, that is exactly how we have it set up for our own families.

Preplanned Funeral Policies

One good option is a preplanned funeral policy. It is a contract with a funeral home to predesign an entire funeral of your choosing, be it burial or cremation. The plan can be paid over time (with interest) or paid in full all at once. Ideally, the policy should be fully transferable and usable in any funeral home across the country.

One major advantage of this setup is that such plans protect against inflation in an industry where prices double every seven to 10 years. The key is to look for guarantees, which means costs are fully covered as described, regardless of what they happen to be once it's actually time for the funeral.

A preplanned funeral policy can protect your family in two ways. First, your loved ones don't have to make decisions at such a vulnerable time because you already made them long before the emotion of the moment. Thus, your family knows that your decisions reflect how you would like to be celebrated. Second, the policy ensures that the financial cost will not be a burden on your loved ones. Everything is already paid for. And no one needs to be worried about making costly mistakes during a time of great grief, which can be quite distracting.

To protect against the few dishonest players in the industry, it is crucial that you make sure you know where the money you pay for these services will be held. For example, it should never be held at a funeral home. Instead, it should be held in a bank trust that earns interest. Or it can be paid into a cash value life insurance policy where it also can grow. The accrued interest is what makes it possible to lock in rates in advance because the interest covers cost increases.

Most of all, a preplanned funeral policy allows your family to celebrate their memories. It eliminates having to focus on the "business side" of the funeral.

In Defense of Hospice

Our family has a lot of experience with hospice. Amy, Skip's wife and Libby's mother, worked in hospice for about seven years. We learned that you can pay anybody to do anything except care about you. As we approach the end of our lives, one thing is clear. The end is the end. Our firm thinks the best approach is to make the experience as positive as possible for the patient and their family.

Hospice care is a special kind of care. It focuses on the quality of life of everyone involved. For the patient, it provides comfortable, compassionate care in the last phases of an advanced, life-limiting illness. For the family, it helps bring some semblance of peace because their loved one isn't suffering.

The philosophy of hospice is unique because it accepts death as the final stage of life—emphasizing "life." No effort is made to hasten death or postpone it. Instead, the goal of hospice professionals is to manage symptoms so the patient is surrounded by loved ones, with dignity and quality of their remaining life being the primary areas of focus.

Hospice can be funded through Medicare Part A once the patient has a life expectancy of six months or less. However, the average stay in hospice is only about seven days, although we think it should be much longer. There is often a reluctance to initiate hospice care because no efforts are made to postpone death. Many families think of hospice care as a sign of giving up. It is not. It's acknowledging the reality that a loved one is near the end of their life on earth.

Hospice is the one path to ensure the patient's life is celebrated and the family is supported to the end. In fact, it's not uncommon for hospice programs to offer support for the family after the patient passes away.

We used to believe that preplanned funeral policies and hospice care made things easier on the family. But our opinion is a bit different now. The fact is that losing loved ones is never easy. We changed our tune when a family we helped pulled us aside at the funeral home and said, "It's not easier. But it was smooth." So now, understanding that losing loved ones isn't easy no matter how much planning is done, we aim to help make things smoother.

When a loved one passes away and the funeral is already planned, there are no hiccups. Then the family can celebrate their loved one's life. Maybe another family member takes a turn for the worse and has to be admitted to a memory care facility. With powers of attorney in place, assets are protected from the nursing home. When they pass away, there's another hiccup-free funeral where life is celebrated. And when it's time for the final settlement of an estate, everything is efficient.

This is exactly what happened with our family (Skip's in-laws and Libby's grandparents). We know firsthand that it was right. It was smooth.

Chapter Seven

NEXT STEPS

Once someone understands the seriousness of protecting their assets and their loved ones with quality estate planning, a sense of urgency seems to take over. Whether it's someone who comes to our office through a referral or because they heard one of our workshops, the next question is always the same: "What's my next step?"

Putting Together a Unique Plan

If you haven't started with estate planning or if the plan you have doesn't protect you against all the fundamental issues we've discussed, your best step is to find professionals with expertise who can put together a comprehensive, personally-tailored estate plan. These are plans that work with your history, your resources, and your dreams.

You worked hard for a long time. Retirement should be fun. You don't want to start every day of your retirement worrying about whether you've made the right decisions or saved enough. Too many families save for retirement and then live cautiously because they think they'll run out of money.

The average age of people we help is 70 years old. Mortality tables from major insurance companies starting at age 70 indicate a person of average health will live into their 80s (age 86 for men and nearly 89 for women). These are the years you want to reap the rewards for all your efforts.

In other words, if you want to eat cake, then eat cake. If you want to take a trip, do it. If you want to treat your grandkids, treat them. If you like a particular type of music, go see it live. Do you have a favorite sports team? Go to the game instead of watching it on TV.

But first, work with someone who will ask all the right questions about your insurance policies, your IRAs, your 401(k)s, and any other assets. Then review how your investments are structured and how you've protected them from the factors that put them at risk such as lawsuits, probate court, nursing home costs, and market fluctuations.

Be sure they help you simplify and consolidate your assets. Also be sure to set up the distribution of your assets when you pass away in order to maximize and multiply them in a way that's simple, easy, and tax-advantaged.

This is our mission for the clients we help. And it should be the mission of whoever you work with as well.

What to Do with Your Money

Many estate planners are content letting you place your money in traditional, unimaginative ways. We don't do that because it will probably lead you to a life you don't want.

Instead, over the past 20 years, we've explored and mastered ways to make the most of what you've accumulated. Here are a few examples.

The IRA Lie

Caring for people who work for you isn't a new idea. Human history offers many examples of organizations that help those who help them. For example, the American government offered surviving Revolutionary War soldiers an income for life. It's called a pension, and the government has made the same promise ever since to those who have served.

As workers moved from the farm to the factory, there had to be a way to care for them after their working years ended. According to the Bureau of Labor Statistics (BLS), employee pensions started with banks and railroads, but in time they spread to most large companies. The government and unions got involved in promoting pensions, and by 1960, BLS data showed that nearly half of the employees working in the private sector had pensions.

Then the government started regulating pensions to protect employees from abuses such as failed or unfunded plans. The Employee Retirement Income Security Act (ERISA) of 1974 created the accountability and disclosure requirements for employer-based pensions and created the Individual Retirement Arrangement (the IRA's original name).

Those accounts were designed for employees of businesses that didn't provide pension plans. IRAs offered some tax advantages and a way to roll the accumulated funds from one job to another.

Over time, the number of companies offering pensions decreased, leaving the responsibility of saving for retirement to workers. As contributing to IRAs was made more accessible, their popularity grew. By early 2021, more than $50.5 trillion was in IRAs belonging to nearly 50 million US households. About 37 million of those households own traditional IRAs.

With traditional IRAs, you put money that hasn't been taxed yet into an account to invest as you see fit. Hopefully, the account grows in value until you're ready to retire. At that point, you can pull the money out to fund your retirement, and Uncle Sam will tax it.

That's what "tax-deferred" means. The government lets you hold the money while it grows. When it's time to withdraw it, you have to pay the taxes. The government even forces you to start that process through RMDs, which are the annual withdrawals you must take or face penalties. We mentioned them in Chapter Two. The SECURE Act 2.0 set the age that those need to begin at 73. It goes to 75 in 2033, and it can always change again.

So what's the problem? Well, the money you thought you had saved for retirement isn't all yours. Instead, you have a governmental partner (or three) in your pocket. Up to half of your money could vanish if you add state and local taxes to the federal taxes you owe on the money you saved over a lifetime.

The traditional IRA plan works great for the government. You saved money so the government could tax those funds at a higher rate in the future. Then when you pass away, anything left in those accounts will go to the heirs you designated. When that happens, not only will they be grieving, but they'll also have the money taxed as regular income when they withdraw it.

This probably isn't the distribution plan you thought you were building for your retirement. What's the alternative? Actually, you have a few options.

You can spend the RMDs you're forced to take. After all, that's probably why the money was saved in the first place. But many families already have their homes paid off by this stage in life. They already drive the cars they want and travel where they want. So they don't need the money and probably won't spend it.

You can give it away. There's always the option of taking the "unnecessary" RMD, paying the taxes, and then donating it to your favorite cause. However, most families are not quite ready to do that—not yet anyway.

A third option is to make a bet you're highly unlikely to lose—you can buy life insurance. It might sound odd, but it works. Instead of spending or donating RMDs, you can take the money out, pay the taxes, and then place the money in a life insurance policy that builds cash value.

When the policy is triggered, the money will be available to your heirs on a tax-free basis. And if they need the money, they can access it as a loan against the policy and pay it back to themselves.

In many cases, this plan can offset most (or all) of the taxes you paid on the majority of the RMDs. Now your IRA is rescued!

A Tax-Free Retirement Plan

We have no issue with paying taxes because it means money was made. Also, taxes fund critical services and infrastructure. After all, soldiers, police, and firefighters need to be paid, just as roads need to be maintained. We'd prefer that those funds come from our income taxes, not from our retirement funds (and you likely would agree).

So we've developed an alternative to ticking tax time bombs that are waiting to go off. Like any other investment, it still requires time and patience. It also requires an open mind.

This traditional IRA alternative starts with saving money regularly, just as with an IRA, except you use after-tax dollars instead of pre-tax dollars. That means you've already paid taxes on the income that's set aside. You'll be giving up the tax deferral advantage of an IRA, but remember, this is an extended play and requires an open mind.

Another difference is where you put the money. In the first quarter of 2021, about 45 percent of the $50.5 trillion in American IRAs was invested in mutual funds.[5] That money is exposed to potentially volatile market risk.

Instead, why not let the brilliant financial minds of the insurance industry put it to work? Here's how. Put your money in a specialized insurance product called an annuity that is not "in" the market but is instead linked to a market index (or multiple ones).

In exchange for letting insurers use the money, you get some wonderful benefits. For instance, you could be credited with any gains the market makes. That said, gains will be capped. Still, the ceiling can be quite high (some contracts offer caps of 13–17 percent, depending on the insurance company).

The real value of this type of insurance contract is that there is also a floor. That means if the market falls, you don't lose value because of investment losses. You might not make anything in a falling market, but in these scenarios, zero is a hero.

---

[5] *https://www.ici.org/viewpoints/22-view-iras by James Duvall Viewed: Aug 2023*

With this strategy, you give up extraordinary gains the market sometimes makes in exchange for protection against market losses. Let's look at an example. Assume your cap is 17 percent. If the market goes up 20 percent, you will be credited with your cap of 17 percent. But if the market drops big like it did in 2022, your credit will be 0 percent (remember, zero is a hero). For retirees, that 0 percent floor is powerful.

We said this was a tax-free retirement plan, right? The accumulation in the account is terrific because it's risk-free with the cap and the floor.

But how do you create income in this strategy? Well, you don't. And you don't want to because income is taxed. Instead, you take a loan from the accumulation value of the contract. That loan will be repaid from the death benefit proceeds built into the contract. Whatever money remains after repaying the loan is then paid to your beneficiaries, tax-free.

There are several other benefits too. For example, unlike traditional and Roth IRAs, there are no restrictions on how much money you can invest with this strategy. These insurance contracts can also be used for college planning far more effectively than 529 college savings plans.

In short, these specialized insurance policies are extremely appealing, tax-free retirement tools, yet very few people take advantage of them. It's because people don't understand them, and many financial professionals don't know how to structure them correctly.

The Child Asset Builder

Understanding the seriousness of estate planning is a big step. It's something you have to want to do for yourself and your family. But too many people live for today and don't think about tomorrow.

As a culture, it's easier to avoid thinking of death than living fully because of it. So a lot of people don't prepare for the consequences of financial decisions. It seems like most people aren't taught a lot about money in school. Likewise, too few parents have discussed money—that taboo subject—or the importance of saving with their kids.

The importance of saving hit home one day when we met a 45-year-old client whose father taught him to save 25 percent of everything he earned, starting with his first part-time job in high school. He's a multimillionaire today, free of most of the financial stresses many of us have felt at different times in our lives. It turns out that he had been given a road map—one that children are rarely given.

Our firm knows the uncertainties of life. It's why we decided to develop a solution to protect kids, no matter where life took them. We call it the Child Asset Builder.

The concept isn't new, but today's technologies and products can significantly enhance it. The Child Asset Builder combines a fast-start savings program with life insurance along with critical, chronic, and terminal illness coverage. This solution allows the policy owner—whether parents, grandparents, or another adult—to use the money as needed while the child grows.

How does it work? Well, let's go over the different parts of the roadmap.

Life insurance costs for young people are typically minimal. You can buy large amounts of coverage as long as at least one parent has the same coverage as the child. If there are multiple children in the family, they all need equal coverage.

One of the best reasons for buying life insurance when someone is young is future insurability. Once approved, that person won't face any underwriting as long as the premiums are paid. That locks in low starting costs, and the child is insured no matter what.

Later in life, the policy can help secure loans, pay down debt, and protect a future family. Since the policy covers critical, chronic, and terminal illness, it's there to use if invasive cancer, stroke, heart attack, or another severe disease appears. In these cases, you could pull cash from the death benefit portion of the life insurance (based on the severity of the situation).

The insurance policy is the risk management aspect of the Child Asset Builder plan. No matter what happens, the plan is self-completing. That's a great benefit.

But the best reason for developing this plan is asset accumulation. That's what many parents and grandparents love. They can pay for limited years or make a single payment and start their young loved ones on a fast track to savings. It's a way to leave a legacy while knowing there's an early start on building assets, and that provides comfort and protection.

Parents and grandparents also appreciate seeing the expenses inside these types of plans. As the years pass, the plan's costs tend to go down rapidly. That doesn't happen with mutual funds or other investment strategies. Those expenses tend to rise with account values.

So how do we structure the Child Asset Builder for clients? We combine all benefits into one policy (an overfunded indexed universal life insurance policy). Many insurance companies offer them. But the policy must have critical, chronic, and terminal illness benefits.

The Child Asset Builder works differently than other types of life insurance. It takes out expenses and then puts the excess premium dollars into bonds and fixed investment instruments. It also buys options on an index (index availability depends on the company). A popular choice is the one-year, point-to-point strategy on the S&P 500. Under this scenario, the insurance company purchases an option that bets the S&P 500 will rise in the next year.

If the S&P 500 goes up, the option is exercised, and you take the gain based on the allowances and limitations in the contract. If it declines, the option isn't exercised, and the money remains safe.

One great benefit is that some insurance companies allow loans where you borrow money from the policy and use its account value as collateral. That lets the account value keep working for your family. Since the loan is not considered income, there are no tax implications. You just need to replace the money as soon as possible.

To be sure, this is a simplified example. In reality, the Child Asset Builder plan is a bit more complex. Still, an experienced advisor can put together such a plan to build a solid asset base for your child(ren) or grandchild(ren) that they can use over their lifetimes.

Putting It All Together

The next concern is how to ensure your child or grandchild will maintain the plan you create. How do you know that after you're gone and they have ownership of the plan, they won't spend every penny?

That's where legacy comes in. Remember how families don't talk about money because it's "taboo"? It doesn't have to be that way. The success of the Child Asset Builder plan depends on the context you build around this lifelong gift.

PRO TIP

One idea is to share your heartfelt feelings and beliefs in the form of a personal note.

We've included a sample letter on page 86 so you can see what we're suggesting.

SKOLNIK RETIREMENT SOLUTIONS

We think the chances are pretty good that kids or grandkids in such a plan will be prudent with the policy and money if you teach them the importance of saving. Remember our client who saved 25 percent of all his income and has done that his whole life? Stories like that are powerful. They bring the value of saving to life and can help kids who have asset bases built by older family members realize that they've been given the gift of a lifetime.

Hey Baby,

If you're reading this, then we must not be around anymore. Don't be sad, we are together and at peace. We love you so much, and will be watching you from heaven. When we were young, we didn't have anyone to help us financially, and we wanted something different for you. We set up an insurance policy to be your personal bank. If you need it, it's there, but don't use it lightly. If you use it, pay it back, and it will be there for your entire life. While we may not be there to offer advice, we trust you to use this wisely. You're a smart person and so talented. We will be watching from above to see where life takes you. When you use this, remember the wonderful times we had. We don't want you to struggle the way we did financially. You'll have plenty of other struggles to deal with that will help you grow, and develop into the great person we know you will be.

We love you forever and always

Gabby & Granddaddy

Whoever this strategy is for, remember that building road maps with a clear path to financial success calls for focus and review. No matter how successful you might be, it's always good to have a guiding hand on your shoulder. And it pays to check on things regularly. That allows for adjustments when needed.

Putting all these pieces in place isn't easy. If it were, everyone would do it and there would be many young people with solid asset bases. Instead, according to the Experian 2020 State of Credit report, the average American Millennial has more than $27,000 in non-mortgage debt. No wonder so many Americans will tell you they're overwhelmed and stressed about their finances. It's affecting even the youngest adults in our country.

How great would it be to take some of that stress away from your children and grandchildren? Consider a Child Asset Builder plan for the young people in your life. It has served our family and countless others well!

Skip sailing with his two daughters, Abbey & Libby

Chapter Eight

EAT THE CAKE, TAKE THE TRIP

After working with so many families for more than two decades, we see a trend. The average person gets married, raises a family, and helps their kids mature into adulthood. Then they focus on their careers to prepare for retirement. After decades of working, saving, and investing, they finally reach the "holy land" of retirement.

But once the regular paychecks stop, they become somewhat paranoid of outliving their nest egg. Why? After hearing they need millions saved and that some regular percentage of it will be needed to live every year, they start to wonder. Have they saved enough? Should they spend less? What about those rising costs?

We think the financial "gurus" feeding the worry of everyday Americans are full of nonsense. A successful retirement isn't about what you have saved or how you spend money. It is entirely about income.

When we work with families, we perform a gap analysis. We look at fixed expenses, including basic living expenses such as a mortgage, insurance, utilities, food, transportation, and so on. Then we examine variable expenses such as entertainment, travel, gifts, and more. We determine the total household income from Social Security, pensions, investment income, and required minimum distributions. Subtracting total expenses from total income reveals the family's financial gap. For some families, there is a surplus of income. And for some there is a gap that must be made up from somewhere.

Most of our families have diligently saved over time. The typical instrument used is a workplace retirement plan such as a 401(k) or 403(b). Often that is converted at retirement to an IRA and used for income.

But again, once those regular paychecks stop coming in, people can tighten up financially. Here's a news flash. When you're retired, you are allowed to pull money out to offset income gaps.

One of our objectives when coaching families in retirement is to free them to spend money. It's been ingrained into our brains that we should save and not spend. But again, fear takes over, and we tighten up.

Listen! Once you have a good grip on your retirement income situation and we've devised a way to handle an income gap without market risk, it's okay to spend your money. So eat the cake. Take the trip. Enjoy your retirement!

Remember, our average client is in their 70s and will live well into their 80s if they are in good health. Let's examine this with more realism. Suppose you're 70 years old and in pretty good health. Perhaps you have 20 years left. That's a lot of time to enjoy retirement, right? Yes, it is. However, we suggest cutting that time in half because when you're 86 years old, you may not want to go on a cruise, travel to Europe, or take long road trips anymore. That puts even more importance on eating the cake and taking the trips during your active retirement years, which are most likely early in retirement.

Now let's make it more personal. Amy's father (Skip's father-in-law and Libby's grandfather) passed away a few years ago at age 83. A few months prior, he would call us when he was having a bad day. We went to see him at his apartment in an independent living facility. After some pizza (his favorite), he opened up to us about his frustrations.

He was 83 years old, lamenting that he didn't do more in his early 70s. Back then, his wife was with him (she had since passed away), he had his health, and he had a few bucks in his pocket. Fast forward to his early 80s, and he mostly sat in a chair and his wife was gone. Yes, he still had money in his pocket, but he was unable to get out of the chair by himself. So the money meant nothing to him anymore. The only joy the money brought was that it let him buy the extra cable television package. But even that was bittersweet because all he could do was watch TV.

His experience solidified our position on eating the cake and taking the trips. If you live long enough, there will probably come a time when you can't do those things anymore (or you won't want to do them). And at that point, our experience suggests that you'll almost certainly regret passing up those opportunities.

If you're worried about leaving less of a legacy, don't be. When you are gone, your family will simply get a few bucks less, and who cares? It's more likely that they'll be happy that you enjoyed your retirement. You worked hard, and you absolutely deserve it. Go ahead! Enjoy yourself! It's one of the best ways to "Finish Strong."

CONCLUSION

There are exciting things ahead for you as you transition from reading this book to making it happen. Now you can look forward to new ideas, positive progress, innovative strategies, and much more. And you will certainly have questions on this journey.

Everyone has questions, and we're here to answer them as best we can. Come into one of our Ohio offices (one in Amherst and one in Sandusky), and we'll answer those questions. You might be saying, "Well, what should I bring to that meeting?" And we will say, "Wait, wait, wait! It's not a meeting. It's just a continuation of what you've learned in this book."

We'll sit down and talk about your questions and where you are on the spectrum of estate planning. We'll tell you if you're already in good shape or if some things still need to be done—things we can hopefully get done for you.

You've Got Questions? We've Got Answers

People always have a lot of questions for us. Sharing some of the questions our clients have had may answer some of yours. Let's take a look.

> ***Question:*** It sounds complicated. How long does it take to get this done?
>
> ***Response:*** Good question. It depends a lot on the complexity of your situation. But it usually takes three or four weeks.

Question: Do I have to change my CPA or financial person?

Response: We really don't know. That's a good question. What we do is work with everybody. If they can do what we need them to do, great! People usually want to do things the way they've always done them, and we ask people to be open-minded.

Question: If I put everything in my son's name, will I be protected from the nursing home and probate?

Response: Yes, you will. It's protected from the nursing home and probate because you don't own it. But here's the problem. If you put everything in your son's name and your son has an accident that he's held responsible for, he'll lose all your stuff. That's not good. And there are other ways to do this.

Question: This sounds really good. What does it cost?

Response: Great question. I don't like surprises in my life, and there's no surprises for the families we work with. It's like a buffet. Once we go through our process and establish your goals, we overlay them on three main objectives (preserve and protect, simplify and consolidate, and distribute easily and tax-advantaged). Then we present a real plan. Like a buffet, you get to choose what you want to do and what you don't want to do. If you just need the five essential documents (Last Will and Testament, General Power of Attorney, Health Care Power of Attorney, Living Will, General/Universal HIPAA Release) we'll set you up with a good attorney, which will cost you a several hundred bucks. If your only concern is probate, we'll do the advanced directives plus probate, which could cost $800 to $1,000.

CONCLUSION

Here's another example. Let's say you need a complete comprehensive estate plan that is 100 percent Medicare compliant and protects things from lawsuits, nursing homes, probate, and market fluctuations (the preservation trust). The attorney will charge around $4,000.

And remember, as we said in the Introduction, if it's not affordable, it's not a solution.

Thank you for taking the time to read this book, and God bless! Now together let's do what needs to be done to "Finish Strong!"

www.ingramcontent.com/pod-product-compliance
Lightning Source LLC
LaVergne TN
LVHW010305070426
835507LV00027B/3445